SWIRL GIRL:
Coming of Race in the USA

TaRessa Stovall

Copyright TaRessa Stovall 2020
All Rights Reserved

ALCHEMY MEDIA PUBLISHING COMPANY

Copyright @2020 by TaRessa Stovall
All Rights reserved by the author

No part of this book may be reproduced in any written, electronic, recording, or photocopying without the express written permission of the publisher or author. The exception would be in the case of brief quotations embodied in the critical articles or reviews.

For permissions and further information contact Alchemy Media Publishing Co., PO Box 7213, Atlanta GA 30357 or info@alchemymediapublishing.com.

Alchemy Media Publishing books may be purchased for educational, business, or sales promotional use contact: www.alchemymediapublishing.com

FIRST EDITION

Library of Congress Cataloging-in-Publication Data
Stovall, TaRessa
1. Non-Fiction
10 9 8 7 6 5 4 3 2 1
Printed in the United States of America
ISBN 978-0-9989300-5-3

Edited by Donald Brooks Jones
www.donaldbrooksjones.com

_____

Cover Design: Alchemy Media Publishing
Cover Art: Brittani Perkins
Interior Design: Alchemy Media Publishing
Publisher: www.alchemymediapublishing.com

*If I didn't define myself for myself, I would be crunched
into other people's fantasies for me and eaten alive.*

Audre Lorde, Black lesbian mother, warrior, poet 1934 - 1992

Prologue

I always knew what I was. But in the summer of my ninth year, I learned that what I was could cause someone to look at me and see something that wasn't there.

My friends and I spent weekends engaged in our warm weather rituals: splashing in Lake Washington at Madison Beach until we staggered ashore, waterlogged and ravenous. We girls spent hours pretending to be mermaids, frolicking underwater while dodging the hands of the neighborhood boys who tried to grab the edges of our swimsuits to peek underneath. We raced each other to the raft, then cannonballed those nasty boys until they left us alone. Rather than lying on the beach to bake color into our skin, we preferred to jump the waves as the sun reflected off the waters to deepen our varying complexions.

Our little group represented the spectrum of Black and Mixed that made up our comfortably working-class neighborhood, from my skin the color of cocoa butter, to Celia's copper, to Sheryl's rich brown, with others falling in between. We recognized our range of backgrounds, but they didn't seem to divide us from each other.

We lived on the same streets, played and fought and made up; sang, danced, jumped rope and played softball and kickball; whooshed down the steep hills on skates and bikes. We shared food and drinks, claiming "bites" before someone called "ban bites," and intoned, "God bless it, devil miss it," as we ingested food that fell to the ground. We played lightweight versions of the Dozens, stopping at the line drawn with "Yo mama…" unless we were ready to tussle. We played past exhaustion, then raced the streetlights and our mama's voices calling us home. Our different-colored parents and skin tones seemed a simple, unremarkable fact of life.

One regular August Saturday in the year of Our Lord 1964, we dragged ourselves from the water as the sun moved down in the sky. Sheryl and I ran into the girls' changing area to use the bathroom before the long hike home. She was washing her hands at the lone rusty sink as I stepped out of the stall, shimmying my blue one-piece swimsuit back up my damp nine-year-old body. I had to yank extra hard to force the first strap over my shoulder. As I moved towards the sink, reaching for the second strap, Sheryl turned and gasped. Startled, I looked up to see her staring at me, her face frozen in shock.

We'd always dressed and undressed around each other without a second thought. Sheryl's expression worried me. I followed her eyes to check the exposed half of my flat chest for a scary bug, blood, or other danger. I twisted around to try to check my shoulders and back. "What's wrong?" I asked. "Why are you looking like that?"

She shook her head slowly. "It's just that…I thought you'd be striped under your clothes. Like a zebra." She sounded puzzled.

I froze, forgetting the strap still dangling and the exposed half of my chest that showed the high contrast between my winter-pale skin and my darkened summer complexion. Sheryl's deep brown skin was lighter under her swimsuit too, but the contrast wasn't as startling or extreme.

I thought you'd be striped … like a zebra.

Yeah, I thought, Black and White. Just like a stupid zebra. I wanted to be angry at Sheryl but I was too stunned to know what to feel or say. What hit hardest was realizing that she'd been seeing me as radically different from herself.

Back home, I stepped out of the tub to assess my naked two-toned body, Sheryl's words seared in my mind. She wasn't a smart-ass. I'd never known her to insult anyone. She was smart, sweet, polite--the peacemaker in our group. I couldn't believe that as close as we were, with all the things we'd shared, she'd been thinking of me as part animal. It was the naïve sincerity of her words that stung the most.

I wondered if Sheryl thought that all of us Mixed kids were striped under our clothes, or just me because I was the palest. I wondered who else might see me that way.

I didn't have the knowledge or the language to make sense of this new conundrum. I just knew how jarring it felt, how it made me want to second-guess everything I'd taken for granted about the people who were close to me. Maybe the differences between my friends and me were more significant than I'd realized. Sheryl never mentioned it again and she didn't act any differently than usual. We never acknowledged her words. But the world shifted in a new direction that day.

The 1790 Census

The concept of race in the USA is political and economic rather than grounded in genetics, biology, or anthropology.

Politics have always driven how the U.S. Census Bureau identifies people's race or ethnicity. Laws, social attitudes, and changing racial demographics impact America's racial categories. They also impact how the federal government uses census data to determine political districts and allocate political, economic, and business resources in housing, education, employment, political redistricting, medical, and other services.

The founding fathers of the USA were very race-conscious. The census started in 1790 when George Washington was president and slavery was in full bloom. United States marshals went door-to-door to interview people and record their responses. The first race-related categories were "White," "free person," and "slave." From 1790 to 1840, most non-White people were categorized as "Colored."

The Census from 1800 to 1860

The next seven census counts took place during the enslavement of Black people. Their racial categories were fairly consistent with the original 1790 census: "White," "free person" and "slave." In the "slave" category, no distinctions were made between Blacks, Mulattoes, Quadroons, and Octoroons.

The 1860 census was the first to separately count the Native Americans who weren't living on reservations. It was also the first census to count the Chinese, many of whom came to the USA as contract railroad workers--but they were counted only in the state of California.

Chapter 1: Sumthin'

The first Thursday in April, 1968 unfolded without any indication that the world was about to turn inside out.

I awoke as usual, silenced the alarm clock next to my bed and scrambled to my feet, still half-dreaming. Jerked my bedclothes into some kind of order. Mumbled a greeting to Mom, washed, brushed, yanked on my clothes and shoes. Combed the knots from my hair and tried to coax the five-textured frizz into a single direction. Gulped down the Cream-o-Wheat breakfast, kissed Mom, bopped my little brother Greg lightly on the forehead for luck, then ran up the hill to grab my friend Dawn for the trek to another day of eighth grade at Meany Middle School.

We were quite a contrast. Dawn was golden, tall, willowy, and stylish with trendy coiffed hairstyles, a mischievous sense of humor behind her winning smile, and an easy grace in response to male attention. I was pale, short, round and awkward with wild dark hair, uneasy with my rapidly-changing body, and tongue-tied around boys. Classmates sometimes compared us to the comic strip characters "Mutt and Jeff."

As on any other school day, we joined the multi-colored mass of student bodies as we rushed to our lockers, then parted ways to make it to our homerooms before the first bell. Morning classes were generic: teachers threw information at us, hoping something would stick, while we pondered the mysteries and distractions of the hormones flooding our bodies. Nature mocked us with the first signs of a Seattle spring outside the streaked classroom windows, daring us not to daydream about sweeter things than math, science, and history. I stared into space, Otis Redding's new hit, "Sittin' on the Dock of the

Bay," dominating my thirteen-year-old brain, relegating the teachers' voices to background static.

A perfectly unremarkable day.

Lunch was generic cafeteria food doled out by Black and Brown women with watchful eyes and patient smiles. After lunch, I made my normal mid-day visit to the girls' bathroom where, after taking care of business, I washed my hands and glanced briefly at my reflection. I saw three chic Black girls—ninth graders who were infinitely cooler and more sophisticated—crowd around me at the mirror. We'd fallen into this periodic ritual without knowing each others' names or backgrounds.

Their attention normally focused on my hair and tips for improving my style options. But today, the tallest one opened with the question that hovered in the background of my life. Sometimes I even managed to forget that the juxtaposition of my skin, hair, and features caused an itch in some people's brains that cried out to be scratched. It was a query that shouldn't have surprised me, but still managed to catch me off guard.

"What you mixed with?" she asked, her hand skimming my hair from the crown to the flip that grazed my shoulder.

"BlackandJew— "

"See? I told you she was sumthin,'" a shorter, browner girl said, reaching to gently move my bangs away from my eyes.

It felt like they were petting me. It wasn't uncomfortable; I just never understood what made people want to put their hands in the unruly mass of protein sprouting from my head.

"Oooooooh," breathed the third girl, a chubby beauty who popped her gum with the precision of a metronome. "Do you know what I'd do with all that hair?"

I braced myself for their warning about the ways my hair might damage my personality. Back when I was seven years old, a group of teen girls in our neighborhood had eyeballed me when my friend Celia and I passed them on the way to the corner store. "Hmph, look at her," they said. "She thinks she's so cute with alla that hair. And she's gonna be stuck up when she gets older, too!" They didn't seem concerned about Celia, who was also Mixed but browner than me with curlier hair. I couldn't see what dangers my hair held, but I became anxious to avoid them at all costs.

I spent the rest of that day worried about the teen girls' predictions. While I wasn't sure how my hair would cause undesirable behaviors, I decided to take preventive measures. That night, I told Mom that the weight of the hair I'd never had cut in my seven years was giving me headaches. My mother watched sadly as the hairdresser whacked off my butt-length tresses, leaving a messy few inches behind. I flinched at my reflection, hoping that looking like a pitiful waif would vaccinate me from future personality flaws. One thing was clear: While I hadn't thought I was cute before, there was no danger of that now.

But six years later, this trio of stylishly-coiffed cool girls in our middle-school bathroom mirror seemed unconcerned about my potential personality deficits. They were just eager to help me turn my multi-textured mane into something more fashionable.

"I could show you some boss styles," the chubby one offered warmly with a dimpled, gap-toothed grin as she teased the crown of her sleek upsweep with a thin comb.

Before I could respond, the bell blared, sending us all rushing out the door.

I forgot about my hair in the struggle to move through the crush of brown, beige, and yellow bodies packing the hallway. I held my books high on my chest to shield my breasts from groping hands while pressing against the wall to keep from getting pulled into the boys' bathroom where rumor had it that girls yanked inside could be gang-raped. We called it running trains. I fast-walked past the danger zone to Miss Caldwell's English class, where I plopped into my seat and set my English textbook and Pee Chee folder on the scuffed desk.

As the class filled with students racing to beat the bell, Ms. Super Cool strode to the desk across from mine. I felt like a sweaty, disheveled disaster next to her, so at ease in her glowing (and pimple-free) brown skin, smiling as everyone greeted her with reverence. No wonder she was always named "cutest girl" and "best-dressed" in the eighth-grade popularity polls. Her smooth hair, coordinated skirt-and-sweater sets and stylish penny loafers put my itchy plaid dress, clunky "corrective" shoes and droopy knee socks to shame. She included me in the beam of her perfect smile, and I squeaked a grateful, "Hey," while betting she didn't have ninth graders offering to give her makeovers in the girls' bathroom. She was too nice to dislike and too perfect not to envy.

"All right class, we're going to review prepositions today. Please open your books," Ms. Caldwell said, tossing her chin-length brown bob as she pointed towards the sentence she'd diagrammed on the blackboard. Like most every teacher I'd ever had, she was White.

"Who knows what these parts are called?" she asked as my hand shot up.

She nodded. "Terri, will you please come up here and show the class how it should be done?"

I marched to the board, outlining the sentence as I spoke. Ms. Caldwell beamed her approval and motioned me back to my seat. Thanks to being a bookworm, I usually knew the right answers. Returning to my desk, I mused that it was nice to feel like I was good at something.

But my brief moment of joy was interrupted by a rough, warm hand sliding up and down the front of my right shin. "Dang! Quit!" I hissed.

Willie sat in front of me, and he reached back to feel on my legs every chance he got. Our desks were so close together that my knees almost bumped the back of his seat. When Ms. Caldwell wasn't looking, Willie leered at me over his shoulder.

Since girls weren't allowed to wear pants to school, my legs were fair game. I studied the contrast between his dark hand and my pale leg, like ink on paper, telegraphing messages that my changing body wasn't something I could protect.

"Stop!" I said when Miss Caldwell moved to the other side of the classroom.

"You know you like it, girl," he'd whisper. Whenever I tried to tell Ms. Caldwell about Willie's roving hand, shame stole my voice. Sometimes he'd wait after class and walk with me. "Keep those big legs sweet for me, hear?" he'd taunt. Other times he'd snap the back of my new training bra as we passed in the hallways, laughing at my impotent rage.

I sighed, doubting that he'd try that mess with Ms. Super Cool.

Willie wasn't the only one. Some of the other boys at school who hadn't noticed I existed the year before had started appraising my changing body with new interest. Increasingly, their hands shot out to grab handfuls of breasts or booty without warning as they walked past.

That day, I vowed to ask about moving to another desk. At the bell, I jumped up and rushed to the teacher's desk. "Um, Ms. Caldwell? I have something to—"

She looked up and smiled. "Terri! I have exciting news. It took a lot of work, but I got you approved to join my Advanced English class! Isn't that great?" Before I could protest that there was nothing wrong that a seat change wouldn't fix, she explained that I was ahead of the other students and would find the advanced class, with its focus on Shakespeare, more challenging and rewarding.

I was torn—excited to be getting away from Willie's intrusive hands, but not sure about Shakespeare. I knew he was famous, but was he as talented as my favorite authors, Langston Hughes and Gwendolyn Brooks? As Ms. Caldwell chattered on, an uncomfortable suspicion gnawed at my mind: Was my skin tone and hair texture the real reason she thought I was "more advanced" and wanted to promote me? She handed me the class change forms for Mom to sign, and I swallowed my suspicion, reminding myself how happy my mother would be at this news. Between seventh and eighth grade, I'd lost all interest in math, science, and history. English was my only hope.

I thanked Ms. Caldwell again, then rushed to my locker to meet Dawn for the walk home, hoping we could stop at Mr. Wong's corner store so I could celebrate with some Red Hots candies. As we walked, Dawn chattered about some new "fine as wine" boy in her math class.

We were joined by a short, skinny, Mixed girl with light brown hair I thought of as Green Eyes. As usual, she ignored me and walked next to Dawn. She got on my nerves, always chasing after Dawn like they were tight.

I followed them into Mr. Wong's store and grabbed my candy, relieved that I had just enough change in my sweater pocket to pay. I stepped outside to wait, savoring the sweet cinnamon candy and wondering about this advanced English class of Miss Caldwell's.

"Hey girl!"

I looked up to see Willie eyeballing me.

"What?" I snapped.

He laughed, white teeth flashing against dark skin. He'd be cute if he wasn't so nasty, I thought, popping another sweet-hot candy into my mouth.

His eyes slid down to my legs. "You know what," he said, moving his gaze up to my breasts.

I stepped back, bumping into Dawn as she and Green Eyes exited the store.

"Hey Willie," Green Eyes flirted, giving her hips an extra twitch as she passed him. "I didn't know you were diggin' on Willie," she said to me when we'd moved out of his earshot.

I pretended to choke on my Red Hot. "Not my type," I said. "He's too—"

"Black?" Green Eyes asked, a sneer edging her words.

"No," I snapped. "He's a nasty poot butt, always feelin' on me. I can't stand him."

"Not everybody likes chocolate," she snickered.

"That's stupid," I said, my voice climbing. "He's straight nasty. That's all."

"Sure, sure, that's what you say," Green Eyes sing-songed, turning the corner towards her house.

At the next corner, Dawn turned to me, her normally jovial face suddenly serious. "What kind of guy do you want to marry? Black or White?"

My mind raced, trying to decode her sudden riddle. "One who's not nasty, okay?"

"That doesn't count. You need to choose," she insisted, her jaw all tight like she was mad with me.

Dawn's strange request made me feel like I was being forced to decide between two flavors I'd never even tasted. I was frustrated by her sudden demand--and my inability to form a coherent thought, let alone fix my mouth to give the right answer. Fighting back tears, I shrugged, turned my back and hurried home to bury myself in the poetry of Langston Hughes.

I'd had enough of being *sumthin'* for one day.

Chapter 2: Only the Good...

The ordinary day continued as late afternoon became early evening. I loved the latchkey hours, with time to myself before Mom and my little brother, Greg, came home. First, I called Mom at Cascade Natural Gas Company, where she worked as an executive secretary, to check in. She asked me to start the rice cooking for dinner around five o'clock, so it would be ready when she got home.

While most of my classmates rushed home to watch the afternoon soap opera, "Dark Shadows," I preferred books, curling up with the poetry of Langston Hughes like a soul starved for jubilation. I dove into the irresistible cadence and imagery of his writing, wondering why they couldn't teach this in school instead of the dead, dry stuff they made us memorize and regurgitate for tests.

I must have nodded off, because the next thing I heard was Mom's key turning in the lock and Greg running downstairs into the house, a burst of curly hair, long lashes, and nonstop energy. He zipped past me to turn on the TV to watch "Speed Racer." Greg had raided the gene pool for our parents' good looks. While I'd been branded the "smart one--thanks both to experts at the University of Washington declaring me "gifted" for being an early reader at age three, and to being skipped from kindergarten to first grade when I was five--Greg was better-looking and actually smarter. It's just that his brand of intelligence didn't always show up in ways that school teachers recognized or rewarded with straight A's.

I rushed to the kitchen, hoping Mom wouldn't notice that I'd forgotten to start the rice. As always, I marveled at how she looked as put-together at the end of a long day as she had first thing in the morning. Her blue-black hair waved softly to her shoulders. Moving gracefully in her stockings and high heels, she tied an apron over her belted, full-skirted dress and sized up the kitchen with her striking blue-green eyes. Then she moved the pepper steak from the fridge into the oven.

I told her about Ms. Caldwell's invitation.

"An advanced class? I like the sound of that," she said, reaching for the forms I was handing her. She skimmed them, nodded her approval, then set them carefully on top of the toaster oven. She called Greg to wash his hands and set the table while she filled our plates with food. We ate the first few minutes in silence. Then Mom asked Greg about school.

He shrugged. "It's okay. I guess."

"What's wrong?" Mom asked.

"This boy keeps calling me names," Greg said, eyes downcast.

"What kind of names?" I demanded.

Greg shot me a glance. My heart sank.

"Is that why you haven't wanted to go to school the past few days?" Mom asked.

"He's older than me. And real mean."

Mom took a deep breath. "Greg, you have to stand up to that stupid boy. If that means you fight him, then you make sure you kick his butt. Or you'll be in trouble with me. Do you understand?"

Greg and I looked wide-eyed at Mom. She'd never told me to kick anybody's butt. He picked at the grains of rice lining his plate. "He's really big, Mom."

"You can't show fear. That's the only way to stop a bully," she insisted. We finished our meal in silence.

As I cleared the table, I wondered what Mom would advise me to do about Willie. Did feeling on my legs and snapping the back of my bra count as bullying? While Mom put the leftovers in the fridge, I ran the hottest water I could stand to wash the dishes. Greg swept the floor and took out the trash, then went into the living room to watch TV.

I washed the dishes and Mom dried, same as always, while we chatted about Ms. Caldwell's opportunity. "I'm really proud of you," Mom said. "I hope you get the rest of your grades up too."

Greg's voice broke in. "Something's wrong! Come see the TV!"

Mom and I glanced at each other, turned off the water, and rushed to the living room. Walter Cronkite's somber face filled the black-and-white screen. "Good evening. Dr. Martin Luther King, the apostle of nonviolence in the civil rights movement, has been shot to death in Memphis, Tennessee."

I knew who Dr. King was, but I wondered what "the apostle" meant. Mom wiped her hands on her apron and sank into the big chair, reaching for one of her Tareyton 100 cigarettes.

"Police have issued an all-points bulletin for a well-dressed young White man seen running from the scene. Officers also reportedly chased and fired on a radio-equipped car containing two White men. Dr. King was standing on the balcony of his second-floor hotel room tonight when, according to a companion, a shot was fired from across the street. In the friend's words, 'the bullet exploded in his face.' Police, who had been keeping a close watch over the Nobel Peace Prize winner because of the Memphis turbulent racial situation, were on the scene almost immediately. They rushed the thirty-nine-year-old Negro leader to a hospital where he died of a bullet wound in the neck. Police said they found a high-powered hunting rifle about a block from the hotel, but it was not immediately identified as the murder weapon."

My body felt chilled as I struggled to take it all in. Walter Cronkite added that the Memphis mayor had put the city back under a dusk-to-dawn curfew, like he'd done the week before when a march led by Dr. King became violent. The governor had called out thousands of National Guardsmen, because police said that the murder had caused acts of violence "in a Negro section of the city."

Then President Lyndon Johnson came on to say, "America is shocked and saddened by the brutal slaying tonight of Dr. Martin Luther King. I ask every citizen to reject the blind violence that has struck Dr. King, who lived by nonviolence."

"Turn it off," Mom instructed, taking a drag on her cigarette before setting it carefully into the ashtray. Greg obeyed her.

"Is it true, Mom?" I asked, my voice shaking.

"What, honey?"

"That only the good die young?" I remembered in fourth grade when my teacher and the principal had burst into tears at the news of President John

F. Kennedy's murder. Mom had shaken her head over and over saying, "Only the good die young."

Mom put her hand on my shoulder. "It seems that way, doesn't it? At least the great ones. Why can't they see that people are just people? One race. Human." She tapped the ashes from her dwindling cigarette and shook her head sadly. "Don't you have homework?" she asked. I nodded, relieved to have an excuse to go to my room and close the door.

I opened my science book, unable to focus on the words swimming across the page. Who cared about the composition of minerals or the anatomy of a frog when the world was falling apart?

I thought about Dr. King, about the flickering black-and-white images of police brutalizing Black men, women, and children with snarling German Shepherds, swinging nightsticks, gushing fire hoses, and tear gas. I admired Dr. King's vision, but wasn't sure nonviolence was the answer to racist attacks. I knew he'd helped to get the civil rights law passed back when I was in fourth grade. His leadership might have helped inspire the change in laws that made marriages like my parents' legal in all states just the year before, when I was in seventh grade. I wondered why there had been so many efforts to keep Black people and White people apart.

Mom never said much about Jim Crow laws, other than to occasionally refer to "down South" as if it were Auschwitz. I despised those Southern racists just as I did German Nazis. Dr. King must have been superhuman to have turned the other cheek in the face of such naked hatred.

Walter Cronkite had called Dr. King an apostle. I grabbed my dictionary: "One sent on a mission … one of an authoritative New Testament group sent out to preach the gospel…"

Mom said that Jews were different from Christians because Jews didn't consider Jesus to be the messiah. Dr. King had been Christian. I wondered if he'd been a racial messiah. And if messiahs had to be crucified because people weren't ready for the powerful goodness they brought to the world.

Head spinning, gut on fire, I pushed aside my homework to scribble a poem.

Mama, what's a nigger?
Why do all the people fight?
How come daddy's face is Black,
and why is mine so light?
Mama, what's prejudice mean?
Who is the KKK?
Why do the kids call me names
at recess every day?
Mama, what's a half-breed?
Is it better to be White?
Why doesn't teacher call on me
when I know my answer's right?
Mama, what's "high yaller?"
Why is my hair so straight?
Mama, what's a honkie?
Is it something I should hate?
Mama, at our school today
Teacher said niggers are dying...
Am I a nigger, too? Are you?
Mama, why are you crying?

Terri Stone copyright 1968

TaRessa Stovall

Chapter 3: There's a Riot Goin' On

Dr. King's assassination sparked uprisings in Black communities around the country. Even before he was gunned down, some cities were exploding with grief and frustration at the ugly outpourings of racist violence. That fateful night, there were even some incidents just blocks away from our house. Young people threw rocks at cars, and some set local businesses on fire. I awoke that Friday unsure what to expect. But Mom ushered us through our normal routine and sent us both to school.

Before noon I was back home, trembling under our kitchen table. The only disaster I'd been trained to handle was an earthquake. I'd never been told what to do when Black and White America collided. Closing my eyes, I replayed the morning's events.

It wasn't raining when I left home that morning, but the spring sky hung dark and ominous. I walked uphill to Dawn's house, tasting the grief and rage in the air. After three sets of knocks, I was about to leave when she stepped out, moving more slowly than usual, her golden face awash with sadness. I was afraid she'd ask me another crazy question, but she was silent. We didn't talk about boys (or hypothetical husbands), annoying teachers or cool songs. We trudged silently past the Catholic girls school, Holy Names Academy, to racially-mixed Meany.

We flowed into the crowd moving through the front doors, the unfamiliar silence eerie. Some of the Black kids looked like they were trying to keep themselves from splitting open. The White kids and Asian kids glanced around nervously. It seemed like the bullet that killed Dr. King had taken a piece out of everybody.

Dawn and I split at the first corner, going our separate ways without even our usual quick wave "'bye." It took forever to get to the homeroom because the back hallway was jammed with people watching a fight. I couldn't see past the crowd but pushed through a chorus of voices screaming "Kick the honkie's ass!" with menacing urgency.

My homeroom teacher, a young White man with a nervous smile and a receding hairline, had the door cracked, eyes scanning the jammed hallway. He grabbed my arm and pulled me into the room, quickly closing the door behind me. "Hurry. Come on! It's safe here."

Puzzled, I slid into a seat.

The teacher's face was mottled with tension. Looking around the room, I realized that he thought I was White and was trying to protect me. As I wondered how to set him straight, a rock crashed through the window and hit him on the shoulder. I jumped up, tore through the door and moved back into the hallway just as a group of tall guys jumped a White boy. People ran in all directions, screaming and knocking each other over.

I heard someone say that the kids from rival Washington Middle School, which had more Black students than Meany, were coming to start fights at our school. I searched frantically for Dawn but couldn't find her. Struggling through the crowd, I pushed my way out the back door to the athletic field, where groups of students and teachers huddled in small groups or wandered with dazed faces and frightened eyes. Mr. Smith, a White teacher, stepped out of the portable where he'd been teaching, to try and quell the rising tensions. He hadn't spoken more than a few words when the wheel of a roller skate came flying through the air and hit him square on the head, causing blood to gush from the sudden wound.

As the chaos grew, I felt more confused than scared. After circling the field, I finally saw Green Eyes and hurried over to her. "Hey, what's happening? Have you seen Dawn?"

She shook her head.

Scanning the perimeter of the athletic field, I saw Dawn's back about 20 yards away. Green Eyes saw her at the same time. I moved in Dawn's direction, but Green Eyes grabbed my arm. I was surprised at the strength of her grip.

"We can't walk with you," she said through clenched teeth.

I shook off her hand and took a step towards Dawn. "I'm serious," she said, her voice rising.

"Who made you the boss?" I demanded.

"People might think you're White," Green Eyes shouted. "We could get hurt!"

I shook my head. "Be for real. Nobody's gonna bother me."

Green Eyes ignored me and ran to where Dawn was standing. She locked arms with Dawn and steered her away, looking over her shoulder to see if I was following them. Too stunned to move, I watched them walk away, their quick footsteps in tandem.

"That heifer has some nerve," I muttered. "She's not that much darker than me."

Then a ninth-grade girl with coloring just like Green Eyes' got jumped by some Washington girls. I started to wonder whether I really was in danger. I moved slowly, looking in all directions, marveling that I seemed to be invisible.

With no other options, I headed home, moving past cars with White parents picking up their children. A group of Washington girls stood in an intersection near Holy Names Academy. They were swinging big metal chains and checking out everyone who walked by. I had to pass them; there was no other way to go.

A few kids from Meany walked ahead of me, single file. The Washington girls scowled as they let the Black kids and a Chinese girl pass. I was behind a shy, blonde White girl from my Home Economics class. I figured her parents hadn't gotten to Meany in time to pick her up in a car. The closer she got to the intersection, the slower she walked, dangling a small beige purse at her side. I stared at her purse, praying she'd get through safely.

The Washington girls stopped the blonde girl, grinning and swinging their chains. Whoosh, whoosh. "Where you going, Blondie?" the tallest girl sneered. My classmate looked around wildly and caught my gaze, silently begging me to save her. I stared without blinking, wishing I could help her, knowing I couldn't.

The girls looked from her to me and back again. The one closest to Blondie grabbed her arm. She whirled away, screaming something, her words a blur under the grey spring sky. They yanked her purse and threw it to the ground. She raised her arm to protect her face, then stumbled away, unharmed, leaving her purse in the street. The girls turned towards me. One of them nudged another. "She White?"

"Don't know," the second one said, looking me up and down for evidence.

The third girl stepped forward, twirling her chain. Whoosh, whoosh! My heart raced. I stared straight ahead, Mom's instructions to Greg fresh in my mind: "You can't show any fear. That's the only way to stop a bully." Their eyes crawled all over me, hoping for a clue. I froze, not breathing, awaiting their verdict, Tina's claim that "people might think you're White," reverberating through my mind. One thing I knew: any claim I made about my identity in this situation would be seen as weakness. I assessed the possibility of getting my ass whupped.

I'd been in plenty of fights, but never with a girl. Boys were easy: you just kicked a shin, kneed a groin, punched an eye or a nose, and then ran like hell. At least that's how it worked before my breasts popped out and my thighs thickened to slow my roll. I'd never dealt with hair and earrings before. My ponytail was sure to work against me, and my skirt wouldn't help either. As I sized up my chances, a soft voice, husky and familiar, came from behind me.

"Hey, Terri." I turned to see Sheryl, looking calm and composed, dimples framing a tight, close-lipped smile.

"Hey," I said, daring to release a small breath.

Sheryl stepped to my side. The Washington girls glanced from her deep brown face to mine and back again, then shrugged and turned to whoever was behind me.

We walked in silence until we reached the corner where I turned left towards our house and she continued down the hill. "Thanks," I called after her, my throat clotted with relief and shame.

She smiled and waved like it was any other day.

I ran up the stairs to our porch, hands shaking so hard I could barely fit the key into the lock and remember which way to turn it. Once inside, I slammed and double-locked the door, then ran to the back door and did the same. I yanked the living room curtains shut and dove under the kitchen table, too shaken to call Mom at her office to tell her what was happening. I longed to change out of my itchy school clothes, and I had to pee. But all I could think about was the chaos outside. I wondered if Greg was standing up to his bully, hating that I wasn't there to help him.

I didn't know what to expect in a real, live race riot. Dr. King's murder had torn my racially-mixed middle school apart. And hate was spilling out onto the normally serene streets of Seattle. Who was a threat, and who was safe?

Would the Black people come for Mom?

Who would come for me? For Greg?

Would our family be forced to turn on each other? Or our neighbors?

What about Dad? He lived a little more than a mile away with his scrawny, sad-faced White wife and her timid daughter. Copper-toned Dad who was quick to insist that he "wasn't Black, dammit." What would he do in a race riot?

I closed my eyes and thought about Dr. King's dream, of his soaring voice and poetic words praying for equality. Justice. To be, as Mom said, "just people."

The urge to pee grew stronger, so I grabbed my knees and rocked back and forth, remembering the recurring nightmare that had haunted my childhood.

I don't know how old I was when I first had the dream or how many times it returned, but it was always the same: Big gruff men in police uniforms loomed outside our house, rounding up everyone at gunpoint—Black people on one side of the street, White people on the other. No other races in sight. No vehicles on the normally busy street. Everything sounded muffled, like when I swam underwater.

I ran down the middle of the street, looking for Mom and Greg. I bit back my rising panic, scanning strange faces in a blur of desperation.

A huge man in an officer's uniform stepped in front of me. "Where are you going?" he barked, lowering his rifle to his side. He towered over me, so tall that I couldn't make out his face. His hands were encased in thick gloves, so I couldn't see his color.

"Where's my mommy?" I screamed. "Where's Greg?"

"Forget about them," he growled. "Just pick a side."

"No!" I shouted. "I don't want to. I don't have to! Just help me find my family." When he didn't respond I added, "please."

He raised his rifle, aimed it at my face, and I froze. "You can't stay here.

There is no middle. Choose. Now. Or else!" he shouted, chilling me from head to toe.

This is where I woke up, heart slamming, sobs heaving, sweat pouring. I got the message: I was supposed to play by their rules, not mine. The same rules Dawn was trying to force on me by asking what color man I wanted to marry.

Dawn. I kept seeing Green Eyes steering her away from me like I was the problem. My blonde classmate's eyes begging me to protect her when I wasn't safe myself. And Sheryl's warm brown face looking like the cavalry coming over the hill. She used her skin to save me. I couldn't do that for Blondie. Green Eyes wouldn't risk it for me.

Finally, I crawled to the bathroom before I wet myself. Then I returned to the kitchen and, staying below the windows, made myself a peanut butter and jelly sandwich. I turned the radio on to "the soulful sounds" of KYAC until it went off the air at sundown, when I switched to KJR, the best White pop station on the dial. From the Temptations to Freddy and the Pacemakers, from Aretha Franklin to Dusty Springfield, I hummed along, wondering at the state of the world.

It was nearly dark by the time I unlocked the front door to let Mom and Greg in. Mom looked tired; for once, Greg didn't rush for the TV. He walked with a slight limp, one side of his face a little puffy with a darkening bruise under his right eye.

His grin lit the room. "I beat his butt," he said proudly.

"For real?"

Mom nodded. "I had to go to the school and talk to the principal, but I got it straightened out. And your brother didn't get in too much trouble."

Maybe they didn't know about the riots. I was proud of Greg for fighting back against being called a "half-breed." My brain hurt from trying to figure out where and how I was supposed to fight, who and what I should fear.

Mom grabbed her apron and began preparing dinner. I stood to join her, stretching my cramped limbs. I thought about Dr. King. He'd stood up, he hadn't shown fear, but in the end, he couldn't kick his bully's butt. Because his bully was bigger than one man with a gun. His bully was the whole USA.

A week to the day after Dr. King was gunned down, President Lyndon B. Johnson signed the Fair Housing Act, which banned discrimination in housing on the basis of color, religion or national origin. In those seven days, riots in more than one-hundred cities across the country left thirty-nine people dead, more than two-thousand, six-hundred injured, and twenty-one thousand hauled off to jail. Seattle had its fair share of outraged violence as well. Cars with White drivers were pelted with rocks and sometimes even overturned. Some businesses in the Central Area that weren't Black owned were damaged. Everybody's nerves were on edge. The possibility of non-violence seemed to have been buried with Dr. King and his dream. And it still wasn't clear whose side anyone was on.

The 1870 Census

This was the first post-slavery census. From 1850 to 1870, a specific "Color" column was added, and U.S. marshals were no longer collecting the information. After slavery ended in 1865, census takers, called enumerators, were hired to determine whether people were full-blooded Blacks, Mulattoes, or other kinds of People of Color.

Racial categories were W for White, B for Black, M for Mulatto, C for Chinese and I for Indian. "Mulatto" included Quadroons, Octoroons, and "all persons having any perceptible trace of African blood."

The 1880 Census

The racial categories were similar to those in the previous census: W for White, B for Black, Mu for Mulatto, C for Chinese (which included all East Asians), and I for American Indian.

Enumerators were told:

"It must not be assumed that, where nothing is written in the "Color" column, White is to be understood. The column is always to be filled. Be particularly careful in reporting the class Mulatto. The word here is generic, and includes Quadroons, Octoroons, and all persons having any perceptible trace of African blood. Important scientific results depend upon the correct determination of this class."

My parents, George Kelly Stone and Rosalyn Weisberg Stone, young and in love, at Madrona Beach, Seattle

Chapter 4: Get Back!

After Spring Break, things had calmed down at Meany. I walked into my first day in Ms. Caldwell's Advanced English class. About a dozen students—mostly White, a few Asian—sat in a tight circle rather than straight rows of chairs facing the blackboard. Ms. Caldwell sat beaming at the edge of the circle. I paused at the door, clutching the thick Shakespeare book, suddenly shy. She introduced me and waved me into one of the seats. A few of the students I knew from other classes shot me quick smiles. Then Advanced English began.

The group leaned into a spirited discussion, joyfully dissecting the intricacies of Shakespeare's plots, characters and lavish language. I struggled to keep up with this level of analysis and discourse, which was far more challenging than graphing a basic sentence on the blackboard.

"Terri, what do you think about the cadence and rhythm of the voices in Macbeth?" Ms. Caldwell asked with an expectant smile.
Feeling all eyes on me, my brain stalled. Ms. Caldwell tilted her head sideways, raising an eyebrow to encourage me. I mumbled something about the complexity of Shakespeare's language, my face hot.

Four other hands shot up. I shrank into my seat, feeling adrift in the rapid-fire discussion, longing for Langston Hughes. I wondered why Ms. Caldwell's regular English class was mostly Black while there was so little color in this advanced class. I couldn't stop worrying that she'd chosen to promote me because she mistook me for White, or thought that my skin and hair made me smarter or more deserving than the mostly brown-skinned Black students in the "regular" English class I'd been in before.

I'd never been in a class where students were encouraged to share their own thoughts and ideas. It was exciting, but at times I struggled to keep up with the intricate plot twists and lofty linguistics of The Bard. The second week in, Ms. Caldwell pulled me aside after class, a look of concern furrowing the skin between her eyes. "Are you feeling comfortable here?" she asked.

"I'm getting used to it."

"Good," she chirped, relief loosening her puckered forehead. "Just focus on the lessons, and I'm sure you'll do fine."

I seized the moment. "Ms. Caldwell? I know you're really into Shakespeare, but could we maybe look at something by Langston Hughes?"

"The Negro poet from the Harlem Renaissance?"

I nodded hopefully.

"Well, it's not in the lesson plan, but if you'd like to share something of his with the class, I could make an exception. You have two weeks to bring it to me. Okay?"

I thanked her, wondering which poem to choose. Maybe I could get away with two.

After the final bell rang, I hurried to the school library to hunt for Langston Hughes books. I checked out one I hadn't seen before and hurried to my locker. As I slammed the door shut, I saw Willie out of the corner of my eye, walking fast and scowling. Behind him were two girls, chanting:

Dark Shadows, black as night
Get on back 'cause you ain't right

I pressed my back against the lockers, trying to make sense of the scene. Both girls had "Black is Beautiful" Afros with medium-brown skin. Why were they rankin' on Willie? Maybe he'd been feeling on their legs or snapping the backs of their bras, too.

Willie walked fast but they moved sped up, steady on his heels, their voices growing higher and sharper:

"You so black that you'd better get back!"

Willie sped up, nearly running, and so did they. I wondered why he didn't turn and make them stop. The girls spotted me and waved for me to join them.

He swung his head around to look dead at me.

I wanted to say something, or shake my head, to let him know I wouldn't do that, even to him. When words failed me, I turned and rushed through the double doors into the fading afternoon sunlight. The slap of my shoes on the pavement brought back the jump-rope rhyme that had perplexed me years earlier.

The older neighborhood girls taught us all the rhymes. Most were funny, like, "Hate to talk about your mama, but you talked about mine. She got a ping-pong booty and a rubber behind ...". But one of the most popular rhymes left me scratching my head:

"If you're White, you're all right." There were no White kids playing with us, but it seemed friendly.

"If you're yellow, you're mellow." I knew that meant me, and I tried to feel grateful.

"If you're brown, stick around." That was most of the other girls.

"But if you're Black, get back! Get back! Get back!" Each word landed like a punch.

My lips froze on the last line, waiting for somebody to protest. But all the older girls--light, medium, and dark--chanted the rhyme with gusto, laughing and nodding.

I'd glance at Celia and Sheryl, light and dark brown. They didn't seem bothered, so I figured this was the code, and I'd better get with it. I danced over, under and between the whirling double-dutch ropes, mouthing the incantation, half-afraid of what it might conjure.

Now that I was in eighth grade, the rules weren't any clearer. I didn't understand the whispers I'd heard that, when it came to boys, "the blacker the berry, the sweeter the juice." I didn't know whether light-skinned people were expected to feel like we were better than the Willies of the world and if so, why we had to make them feel bad to make ourselves look good. It didn't seem right to attack anyone, even nasty poot-butt Willie, for the way God made them.

A few weeks later, the three ninth-grade girls crowded around me in the bathroom again, all sporting big Afros. Now they weren't admiring my hair.

They were laughing at it.

"You can't get a natural with that stuff, can you?" they teased, fluffing out their crowns.

"Yeah, Black is Beautiful, baby!"

"Right on!"

Everything but my hair had changed. Dawn and Green Eyes got Afros, holding their heads extra high. Then Greg announced that he was getting one too. I prayed for mine to grow up and out like his, but God wasn't listening.

I retreated into my books, looking through the new Langston Hughes collection I'd grabbed from the school library. I scanned the pages, seeking the perfect poem to share with Ms. Caldwell's Advanced English class.

I found one that I'd never seen before, titled "Cross." In it, Hughes wrote a lament from the perspective of a Mixed-race person born to an impoverished Black mother and a well-to-do White father. He didn't hint as to whether the Mixed person was conceived via rape, consensual sex, or something in between. The poem ended with the Mixed person wondering where they'd die since they didn't fully belong to either race.

I was hurt by this trite, stereotypical portrayal that equated being Mixed race with being confused, and deeply disappointed in my favorite author for perpetuating the "tragic Mulatto" in his work. After reading the poem over and over, silently and aloud, I threw the library book to the ground, jumped up and hollered, "I thought you were the best, Langston Hughes. I loved you so much!"

I talked to him as if he were alive, though I knew he'd died the year before. The librarian had told me, her long hazel eyes wet with sadness. "He's gone," she whispered, sliding one of his books across the counter to me. "But his works live on."

Once my emotions cooled, I grabbed a pencil and tore a sheet of paper from my notebook:

Uncrossed

Sometimes you call us half-breeds

Say we don't know where we belong

Where to laugh or cry, live or die--

Sorry, but you've got it wrong

Just because my mom and dad

Are from different races

Doesn't mean that I'm confused

Or wear conflicted faces

It's easy to look down on us

From your perch on high

But we're too busy living

To wonder where to die

Contrary to what you think

We're not all defined by strife

Mixed blood is no cross to bear

It's just a fact of life

Terri Stone copyright 1968

I looked up toward heaven where I knew Langston Hughes resided, called his name, and read the poem aloud three times. Even if he didn't care, I wanted him to know how I felt.

Chapter 5: By Any Means…

America was still adjusting to life without Dr. King when I unexpectedly encountered a voice that rocked my soul.

Mom's younger sister, Auntie Shirley, had flown in from Minneapolis to visit us for Mother's Day. When I woke up on Saturday, they were drinking coffee at the kitchen table, talking in low, urgent voices.

They didn't look anything alike. Auntie Shirley was shorter than Mom with huge dark brown eyes and a large, stereotypically Jewish nose. Ironically, her hair was kinkier than my father's. Mom confided that her sister used to go to Black hairdressers in their North Minneapolis neighborhood to get it straightened. It wasn't fair, I thought, even she got to have an Afro, and she probably didn't even want one!

While Mom was practical, serene and down-to-earth, Auntie Shirley was intense and mysterious, with an otherworldly aura. Mom said she was psychic. Years before, during dinner in her suburban Minneapolis home, she nonchalantly said that I'd been one of President George Washington's Mulatto slave children in a previous life. Then she turned and asked Greg to pass the bread.

Mom, the middle child of five, was close to all of her siblings, but had a soft spot for Auntie Shirley, nicknamed "Baby." I greeted her with hugs and kisses, answered the usual questions about school, feigning excitement about my promotion to Ms. Caldwell's Advanced English class.

Auntie Shirley smiled her approval, then gestured to a paperback book sitting on the kitchen table. I didn't recognize the Black man's face on the cover.

"This is a very powerful book," Auntie Shirley said. "It's positively brilliant. But there is some controversy—he calls White people devils."

I couldn't take my eyes off the book "Who is that?"

"It's Malcolm X, dear. A colored leader—"

"It's Negro now, Baby," Mom corrected gently.

"Like Dr. King?" I asked.

"Not exactly," Auntie Shirley said. "But brilliant in his own way."

"May I please read it?"

Auntie Shirley looked to Mom, who glanced at me. "I'll write an extra credit report on this for Advanced English," I promised.

Finally, Mom nodded and Auntie Shirley handed me the book, looking even more serious than usual. "Just don't forget your Jewish side!"

"Thanks!" I said, not sure what she meant by that last remark and wondering why she was reading this book in the first place.

I devoured The Autobiography of Malcolm X, stopping only for quick meals and bathroom breaks. No other writer, not even Langston Hughes, had pierced my heart and mind with such white-hot precision. This must be how people felt when they read the Bible, as if somebody flipped a switch that shone light into all of the darkness. Malcolm X awakened deep insights, spoke to my truths and finally—finally—gave me the tools to make sense of the world into which I'd been born.

I normally zipped through a book a day, but I took my time with Malcolm X, savoring each word, holding each idea up to the light for further examination. I analyzed my own questions and feelings against the backdrop of his journey, as if he alone understood the emotions and questions that plagued me. I wanted to flee to wherever Malcolm X lived and beg him to adopt me so I could sit at his feet and absorb his wisdom.

I read the book twice straight through, but it wasn't until the second time that I noticed the epilogue. My heart splintered as I read about my new hero's murder in New York City three years before. Unlike Dr. King, Malcolm X's killers had been Black.

I collapsed, sobbing, my fantasy of a mythical Black father destroyed.

Had Malcolm X been an apostle or a racial messiah? I wondered what he and Dr. King were talking about in the afterlife.

Malcolm X's words ran through my mind as I stepped into Ms. Caldwell's class. "We'll be ready for your Langston Hughes presentation tomorrow," she told me. "So please make sure you're well prepared."

"I found another writer I'd rather share. Malcolm X. May I please talk about him instead?"

"I've never heard of him. Is he a poet or playwright? From the Harlem Renaissance?"

I shook my head. The bell rang. "Let me think about it," she said.

We discussed "A Midsummer Night's Dream," and Shakespeare's concept of a "winged Cupid painted blind."

But all I could think of was Malcolm X's words about our country's racial climate and how his approach to challenging racism compared with Dr. King's.

I jumped when Ms. Caldwell called my name. "Terri, what do you think about that passage? How would you interpret his words?"

I slid way down in my seat. "I don't see the point of spending all this time on an ancient dead man whose writing has no relevance to my life."

I was surrounded with wide eyes and shocked silence. Ms. Caldwell did a double take, shot me a quick glare, and moved on to another student. After class, she approached me. "Can you please tell me what is going on?"

"I know you worked hard to get me into this class. I appreciate it. But can I please go back to your regular English class?"

She looked defeated.

"Please."

She nodded without speaking. I thanked her. "I'll take care of the paperwork," she said.

Mom wasn't happy. I felt bad about letting her and my best teacher down, and ashamed that I wasn't as "advanced" as they'd hoped. I couldn't shake the feeling that Ms. Caldwell had promoted me because of my color. Mom always said I was smart, and I believed her. But I wondered who else would see me that way if my skin was darker, my hair curlier and my features more rounded.

The next day, I was back in the old classroom. The only empty seat was behind Willie. Ms. Caldwell didn't look to me for any of the answers, and though I knew them all, I no longer bothered to raise my hand. Listless, I doodled on my Pee Chee until I felt a cold hand on the front of my leg.

"Quit, Willie!" I growled, surprising myself with the venom in my voice. And for the very first time, he did.

The 1890 Census

Racial categories in the 1890 census were increased to include color, tribal status for Native Americans, and more specific Asian national origin groups. In an attempt to drill down in identifying Black people, this was the first census to specify a blood quantum for categorizing Black or Mulatto. The enumerators were instructed to:

> Be particularly careful to distinguish between Blacks, Mulattoes, Quadroons, and Octoroons. The word "Black" should be used to describe those persons who have three-fourths or more Black blood; "Mulatto" those persons who have from three-eighths to five-eighths Black blood; "Quadroon" those persons who have one-fourth Black blood; and "Octoroon" those persons who have one-eighth or any trace of Black blood.

This was also the first census to identify all individuals having any trace of Indian blood--some Mexicans might have been counted as Indians in previous census counts--and the first census to formally tally Japanese people.

TaRessa, age four

Chapter 6: Yiddish and Jazz

Some people say that babies and small children "don't see color," but as far back as I can remember, I've catalogued people's identity according to their hue, straining to make sense of the dynamic that defines so much of our world. As a child, I'd study myself in the mirror, trying to trace the journeys of my ancestors in my mismatched coloring and features.

Before they were my mother's parents, Eva Stein and Louis Weisberg were children in Odessa, Russia, growing up Jewish under the shadow of constant threats and persecution. They didn't know each other, but both immigrated to the United States in hopes of better opportunities and an end to the horrors of the pogroms.

Eva was a petite beauty who hailed from the peasant class, with raven hair, wide dark eyes full of curiosity and a pouting cupid-bow mouth. She was about four or five years old when her mother, Brina, father, Sam, and seven brothers and sisters came to the states through Ellis Island and landed in the Jewish immigrant community in Duluth, Minnesota. Despite their last name, the Steins did not claim any German ancestry.

My grandfather, Louis Weisberg, was tall, lean and aristocratic, from an upper-class family; his only sister was a doctor. Louis had lustrous dark hair and soulful eyes. His very full lips hinted at some North African Jewish ancestry. He was an ambitious adventurer who left most of his family to travel alone to the United States at just seventeen years old. After being processed through Ellis Island, he ended up in Minnesota, where his only brother, Sam, lived in St. Paul.

Since Eva had come to the United States as a very young child, she spoke fluent English, and grew up to work as a translator. She met Louis in Duluth, Minnesota, when he enlisted her linguistic services. Duluth had a vibrant Jewish community comprised of German, European and Eastern European Jews, including Russians, who came to this faraway land seeking sanctuary and hope. The small size of Duluth's Jewish community minimized tensions between the groups. My grandparents married and had three of their five children there: Kenneth, Beatrice, and my mother, Rosalyn. In 1924, when Rosalyn was just a year old, the family relocated to North Minneapolis, where the younger siblings Merton and Shirley were born.

Black people and Jewish people lived side by side in North Minneapolis, partially because both groups were shut out from other parts of the city. Their shared status as marginalized people on the low end of the socio-economic ladder created a sense of camaraderie which enabled them to coexist in relative harmony.

While some of the Jewish people changed their names to assimilate into better opportunities, Louis held fast to Weisberg and chose the entrepreneurial path as a salesman in the garment trade. Eva struggled to manage the household and five children, battling the depression that sometimes left her unable to get out of bed for several days at a time.

Though Louis was a gifted salesman, the uncertain income left the family teetering between feast and famine. Sometimes they could afford a maid; other times, they barely scraped by. When times were lean, Eva pulled herself together and played poker with the other Jewish women in the neighborhood, where she won enough money to feed her family for another week.

Eva and Louis's middle child, Rosalyn, was a shy, soft-spoken cherubic beauty with a round face, ink-black hair, and twinkling turquoise eyes. She loved school, but couldn't always attend because the lone school outfit she hand-washed was slow to dry in the Minnesota cold. When her mother's depression left her unable to function, Rosalyn—the second of three daughters—stepped in to cook and clean for the family. She learned to create delicious meals from scraps and maintain a sparkling house, earning her the nickname "Little Mama" and a lifelong penchant for feeding and nurturing everyone she met.

As young Rosalyn hit puberty, she became smitten with her older brother Kenneth's best friend, a handsome Negro named George Stone, nicknamed Kelly. He was an accomplished tap dancer with big, soulful eyes, a one-sided smile, and more than his fair share of charisma and charm. She kept her growing crush a secret.

Kelly was born in Des Moines, Iowa, seven years before Rosalyn, though they shared the same mid-September birthday. His mother, Frances Ursula Johnson, was one of seven sisters born to L.H. and Alice Johnson in Marshallstown, Iowa. In her late teens, Frances, a light-skinned, long-haired young woman of Black, Native American and German ancestry with an air of melancholy, married Vernon Warness Stone, a slender, handsome barber a few shades darker than herself. Vernon was the eldest of three sons born to Izaelia Yerby Stone and Kelley Stone in Kingston, Missouri.

Frances and Vernon had one child, a son, named George Lewis Stone, who was called Kelly after Vernon's father. I don't know why the "e" in Vernon's father's name was dropped when it became George's nickname. The family moved to North Minneapolis when Kelly was a child. From a young age, Kelly was fueled by a single dream: to be a professional dancer. He dropped out of school after eighth grade and tap danced around North Minneapolis, earning praise and money for his smooth moves and buoyant charm.

Kelly shared his dancing talent and dreams with his best friend and dance partner Katie, a stunning dynamo with a similar coppery skin tone and blended Black and Native American heritage. One fateful day, the teenagers gave into their hormones, and Katie became pregnant. They married, Katie put her dancing dreams on hold, and a beautiful baby girl named Shirley Carolyn was born to the young newlyweds.

But Kelly wasn't ready to settle down and fully commit to family life. After years of tumultuous ups and downs, he and Katie divorced but remained friendly for the sake of their daughter, Shirley. When Kelly's acrobatic dancing feats damaged his knees, he channeled his rhythmic gifts into jazz drumming.

To earn a steady paycheck, Kelly joined the ranks of African-American men working as Pullman porters on the nation's train system. George Pullman, an industrialist who was instrumental in creating the world's first sleeper trains, formed the Pullman porters as servant-like attendants to make the well-to-do, usually White, travelers more comfortable. The first Pullman porters hired were formerly enslaved Black men. The work was demanding and demeaning, with long hours and low pay. The porters weren't allowed to attend to Black guests riding in segregated train cars. Though Pullman porters were highly respected in the Black community, at work they suffered many forms of discrimination. The racist Whites who insisted on calling all of the Black men working as Pullman porters by the name George caused Kelly to hate his legal first name. He changed his middle name to Kelly to make his nickname official.

Maternal Grandparents: Louis and Eva Weisberg

TaRessa Stovall

Meanwhile, Rosalyn's adventurous spirit caused her to flee Minneapolis as soon as she graduated from high school. She headed to sunny California, where by day she worked as a retail clerk in clothing stores, and nights and weekends as a hatcheck girl in some of Los Angeles's most popular nightclubs. There she saw and waited on some of her favorite movie stars including Lana Turner, Clark Gable, Ava Gardner, and Spencer Tracy. Craving even more adventure, she became one of the first women to work in the San Francisco Naval Shipyards during World War II. Along the way, she connected with her brother's friend and childhood crush, the dashing Kelly Stone.

Kelly might not have remembered Rosalyn as a child, but he was drawn to the classy beauty with the regal cheekbones, trim hourglass figure, and subtly seductive smile. They shared a love of good jazz, dancing, and fashionable attire. Kelly sported the dramatic zoot suits favored by Black, Latino and Italian men and jazz musicians who wore them as hip badges of cultural pride. Rosalyn stayed equally sharp with her sleek black pompadour hairstyle, chic fashions, and flawlessly coordinated accessories. Rosalyn turned down several devoted, wealthy White suitors because she stubbornly believed that her romantic destiny was with Kelly Stone.

They landed in Seattle in the late 1940s, a place for people seeking fresh starts and new horizons. Washington state didn't have any laws against interracial marriage (though attempts had been made years earlier), and the tolerant atmosphere drew many who found love across the color line.

While it wasn't as high profile as Harlem, Chicago or other well-known jazz cities, Seattle had a vibrant jazz scene. Its heyday was between 1937 and 1951, when Boeing Industries made the city a player in the defense industry. That, coupled with soldiers from Fort Lewis in nearby Tacoma, turned Seattle into a hotspot for jazz musicians. The heartbeat of the jazz scene was in the Central District just east of downtown, where the polite form of housing segregation called redlining "allowed" most Black people to reside.

"In 1948, there were over two dozen nightclubs along Jackson Street, where jazz and bootleg liquor flowed freely … the scene that nurtured the early careers of Quincy Jones, Ray Charles and Ernestine Anderson," writes longtime Seattle jazz reporter Paul DeBarros in his book, *Jackson Street After Hours: The Roots of Jazz in Seattle*. The atmosphere was as festive as Mardi Gras, with some musicians carrying their instruments from one club to another in search of the hottest jam sessions.

Though these clubs were frequented mostly by Black people, all races were welcome. "The easy give-and-take between the races in Seattle's nightlife district had a profound influence on music," DeBarros writes. "Barriers between Black and White traditions were never as clear-cut as they were in other western cities like Los Angeles, where a "cool" White school evolved in contradistinction to the "hard bop" played by Blacks. In Seattle, the music of both Blacks and Whites tended to merge toward an agreeable middle, resulting in a melding of traditions that later was felt worldwide in the work of Jackson Street denizens such as Quincy Jones, Ray Charles, and Bumps Blackwell."

The sizzling *bohemian* atmosphere was the perfect backdrop for interracial couples who frequented many of these clubs. When Kelly wasn't playing drums, he and Rosalyn showed out--doing the jitterbug and other popular dances. Many of Seattle's Black jazz musicians dated White women (Rosalyn seemed to be the only Jewish one), and they formed a tight community, buying homes near each other in the Central District. The men worked day jobs to support their families, then played gigs and hunted for jam sessions after hours.

The women in these controversial relationships left nothing to chance. In the days before birth control and reproductive choice, my mother and her friends strategically planned their pregnancies so that their little Mixed children would have friends their age, and could build a sense of identity among families that looked like theirs. These dynamics created my community of what I call Jazz Babies—born to nonconformists who had the foresight to band together. This community extended beyond Seattle to family friends in Minneapolis and Los Angeles.

After living together, Rosalyn and Kelly wed on July 21, 1951, in the local courthouse. Their friends and wedding witnesses, Helen Jorgensen and Winfield King, married and bought a house across the street. Eventually, they had two Jazz Baby daughters; the younger, Celia, became my surrogate sister and closest friend.

Around the time that Rosalyn and Kelly married, Kelly's daughter Shirley back in North Minneapolis had grown into a pretty teenager who caught the eye of a "bad boy" at school. Her mother Katie wanted to get Shirley out of the danger zone. She asked around about Kelly's new wife, Rosalyn, and evidently got good reports, because soon Shirley arrived in Seattle to live with her father and the Jewish woman he'd married. Kelly enlisted in the Coast Guard and worked as a Merchant Marine, while Rosalyn leaned on her "Little Mama" experience to take Shirley under her wing. With Kelly gone for long stretches of time, Rosalyn and Shirley formed a close, almost sisterly, bond.

While Shirley was attending Garfield High School, Kelly introduced her to a good-looking, upstanding young Army man named Ralph Pierce.

They fell in love, and Shirley left school to marry and begin working towards her goal of having a big family—seven children, to be exact. She and Rosalyn became pregnant around the same time and Shirley's first son, Ralph, Jr., nicknamed Rocky, was born two months before me.

Since Shirley was an adult when I was born, we didn't know each other as siblings, and I was too young to understand the intricacies of our family dynamic. She was like a cool young aunt or a slightly older cousin with a pretty face and sweet smile who babysat me from time to time.

My father had a reputation for philandering. When I was two years old, and my mother was pregnant with Greg, Mom finally had enough and got a divorce. To her credit, she kept us rooted in the Jazz Baby community.

In the 1950s, when interracial marriages were still illegal in sixteen states, legalized Jim Crow segregation ruled the South, and a more subtle form of racism flourished in the North, we Jazz Babies represented something that wasn't supposed to be. Nobody had to explain that to us; we understood it in the ways that people looked at us and our parents. Even before we could put words to it, we saw the sidelong glances, heard murmurs under the breath, and felt the vibes of disapproval, even in our famously "liberal" and "tolerant" Pacific Northwest homeland.

Being Jazz Babies gave our Mixedness a sense of normalcy. In that small, controlled environment, we were the rule rather than the exception. This knowledge fortified us when we stepped into the wider world where most families didn't look like ours.

Mom's closest friends in this community were Marian and Ernie Hatfield. Ernie was a gifted swing-jazz pianist who had traveled with Ella Fitzgerald as part of her band, The Four Keys, in the early 1940s. Ernie was born in Chester, Pennsylvania, and formed the band with three classmates. They were popular in and around Philadelphia and had a weekly radio program featuring spirituals. While playing a local gig, Ernie was taken by a pretty young German-American woman named Marian who sauntered up to his piano, introduced herself and announced that they were meant for each other. Captivated, he came to agree and soon they married and had a young son. An opportunity to play music drew Ernie to Seattle. Once he decided it was the place to stay, he got a job as a mechanic at Boeing and sent for Marian and their baby to join him.

Marian and Ernie seemed an unlikely couple, even in the Jazz Baby community. She was a sheltered, devout Catholic from a tight-knit family in Wilkes-Barre, Pennsylvania who never learned to drive and whose only work outside the home was volunteering at St. Joseph's, the Catholic church and school up the hill from their small home. When I was little, I couldn't pronounce Marian, so she became "Mamie," while we referred to Ernie as Uncle Ernie in acknowledgment of our extended family bonds.

Like my mother, Mamie was a wonderful cook, and she often fed us when our money was tight. Each year, we enjoyed Thanksgiving dinners and Christmas celebrations at their house. Mom brought her collard greens, candied yams and black-eyed peas, much to Uncle Ernie's delight. Seated at the head of the table, he'd entertain us with wry jokes and memories of his musical exploits. After dinner, he'd duck into his room to change into an elegant suit or tuxedo to play a gig. Before heading out to thrill the crowds at the posh Seattle Tennis Club or one of the upscale hotels or private parties around town, he'd pause to delight us with a mini-concert in the living room, playing our favorite tunes. Mine was "Satin Doll."

When we traveled to Minneapolis or Los Angeles, Mom took us to visit Jazz Baby families, which again reaffirmed our sense of self. If others who didn't understand the Jazz Baby dynamic suggested that we were strange and should be outcasts, we had a frame of reference to refute that perspective. When outsiders accused us of being confused about our identities, we were equipped with the tools to prove them wrong. Some of the couples in our community stayed married; others did not. Sometimes our Black fathers stayed involved with our lives; others—like mine—hung vaguely around the edges. But even a lack of presence or participation couldn't wipe out the music they'd poured into us.

It took me years to realize that in addition to racial and ethnic DNA, I was made of swing-jazz keyboards, soft drum brushstrokes, tapping feet, jitterbugging, around-the-clock jam sessions, blues in the night, and improvised rhythms that invented themselves as they went along.

Chapter 7: Imitation of Life

I hated the popular movie "Imitation of Life" with a passion that defied words. But I never dreamed that the mere mention of it would drive me to violence.

The sappy racial melodrama was one of Mom's favorites. She always enlisted me to watch it with her whenever it came on TV—both the black-and-white 1934 original and the full-color 1959 remake with her favorite actress, Lana Turner.

I was five or six the first time I saw the movie. It was the original version. I was intrigued, because I'd never seen a movie about racial identity, and the main character, Peola, played by Fredi Washington, looked kind of like me—another first. But as the story unfolded, I felt sick to my stomach at the way that Peola hated and rejected her Black mother and the blackness within herself. The remake, which we watched years later, was even worse—Peola's name had been changed to the less ethnic Sarah Jane, and the character was portrayed by an actress who was White and Mexican. I stifled my disgust, cursing Peola / Sarah Jane as Mom sobbed through the tearjerker. I figured I had to suffer through it as some kind of penance for being light-skinned.

As eighth grade sputtered to an end, I was thrilled to qualify for my first summer job, even though it didn't pay a cent. At 13, I was old enough to be a Counselor-in-Training, or CIT, at the downtown YMCA where Greg and I had spent most of our youthful summer days while Mom was at work.

My supervisor was a young man named Ben, a dark-skinned transplant from Chicago with a short Afro. He had great taste in music--we both loved Junior Walker and the All Stars' hit, "What Does It Take?--and he loved to tease me about "talking proper."

One day he said he'd brought a "ham sammich" for lunch. I rushed to correct him. "It's sand-wich! Not sammich—that's not even a word!" "You don't know what you're talking about," Ben teased. "It's sammich." "Sand-wich," I insisted repeatedly. We went back and forth like that for weeks, with Ben muttering "sammich" under his breath whenever he was near.

One July evening, Mom popped popcorn and asked me to watch "Imitation of Life" with her. I did my daughterly duty, stuffing my face and groaning inwardly. I suffered as I watched the White characters exploit the Black woman. I squirmed at Peola for denying her truth to debase herself for the love of a White man and acceptance by a society that deemed her inferior and unworthy.

I'd heard about Black and Mixed people passing for White, but had never seen it up close. I knew that some people passed for practical reasons, like those who faked being White to get jobs, returning to their true identities and communities after hours. That wasn't a sick form of denial or rejection—that was taking advantage of an unjust system.

Mom told me about Dad's Aunt Alice—who I sort of resembled—and her decision to protest racism by eating in a segregated diner on a visit down South. She sashayed in with her glamorous, high-yella, ponytailed self, ordered the most expensive item on the menu, and ate extra slowly, savoring every bite. When a smiling waitress handed her the bill, she pointed to the "Whites Only" sign, saying, "You just served a Negro!" and flounced out without paying for her meal. That was the kind of passing I could relate to.

Her love for "Imitation of Life" aside, Mom didn't seem to have much tolerance for people who denied their identities. She was always pointing out famous Blacks and Jews who were thought to be White or gentile. "She's Black," she'd say about Carol Channing, Dinah Shore, and others. "He's a Yid," she'd reveal about Kirk Douglas, Shari Lewis, Tony Curtis, Lauren Bacall, Leonard Nimoy, and those who she suspected had changed their names either strictly for show business reasons, or to downplay their ethnicity. While there was no way to verify Mom's claims of their backgrounds, I got the message: denying your parentage or true identity was the lowest, most despicable thing imaginable.

That summer day after watching the movie with Mom, I was at work rounding up the younger kids for a YMCA field trip when Ben tapped my shoulder.

"Did you see 'Imitation of Life' last night?" he asked eagerly.

"Yeah." I rolled my eyes, ready to explain why I hated it.

Before I could speak, he stepped closer and said, "You remind me of the girl. What's her name? Peola? Yeah, that's it."

My vision flared red, my brain flooded with heat and my gut hardened into a rock. The next thing I knew, I'd punched Ben in his eye. Hearing his yelp of pain and watching his skin start to swell, I stared, horrified, at my evil hand, scrambling to apologize.

I felt even worse when I was called into the boss' office and put on CIT probation, with strict orders not to mess up again. I kept apologizing to Ben, who shrugged and said, "it's cool." But he kept his distance after that.

I wanted to know more about what made me punch Ben. Unsure how to name it or tame it, I wondered when and where that impulse might pop up again and what it would make me do.

Not long after that, Mom told me how, after Greg was born, her siblings encouraged her to mask our racial identities. Once they saw that Greg was almost as light-skinned and ethnically ambiguous-looking as me, they suggested that Mom move to Hawaii, where she could raise us as vaguely blended without the pesky complications of that Negro stuff. They even offered financial assistance to help her start a new life.

But she wasn't tempted. "I knew we might struggle financially, but I couldn't lie to you and Greg. You have to live your truth so you can face yourself in the mirror. Being Mixed is nothing to hide or be ashamed of," she said.

When Mom left Minneapolis for California as a teen, her elegant beauty attracted many job offers from men. Many of them encouraged her to change her name from Weisberg to "something less ethnic." Some even offered to help her get her nose "fixed." She told them "No thank you," and walked away, keeping her name, her nose, and her integrity intact.

I didn't want to deny my truth, either. But at age thirteen, I didn't know how to weave all the parts of myself together in a world where race, color and identity were shifting so fast it was hard to keep track.

Paternal grandmother, Frances Ursula Johnson Stone

TaRessa Stovall

Chapter 8: Power to the People

The summer of 1968 was a defining season for the whole country. Hostilities still brewed from the anguish of Dr. King's assassination. Young people were noisily protesting the Vietnam war and the draft that forced young men into service. Some White women whipped off their bras to burn them in the name of women's liberation.

The Civil Rights Movement, which had pushed the government to change laws for the better, gave way to the brasher, more in-your-face Black Power Movement, which demanded respect and equality without apology or compromise. This new energy came with bold declarations of Black pride and Black beauty to turn the idea of White superiority on its head.

The blood of leaders continued to flow. The nation was still recovering from Dr. King's assassination when, just two months to the day after he was felled, Robert F. Kennedy, brother of the late President John F. Kennedy, was assassinated in Los Angeles as he won the California primary for the upcoming presidential election. Only the good die young.

Seeing so many leaders gunned down made the quest for racial progress seem as dangerous as it was necessary. There didn't seem to be a blueprint for how to make a difference and survive.

Dawn and I were hanging out one Saturday in August, speculating about the upcoming school year: how to get the coolest ninth-grade teachers, which boys were crush-worthy and which girls had the most boss styles. We practiced the latest dance steps until we were bored, then let Dawn's older sister style our hair and show us what we looked like with make-up, which we admired before scrubbing our faces clean. With nothing left to do, Dawn suggested that we go hang out with her cousins. I agreed, not sure who these mysterious cousins might be. Dawn didn't give any clues as we walked south to the corner of 23rd and Union, then turned east and walked up the hill to 34th Avenue into the Madrona neighborhood. I was starting to think that Dawn had invented these cousins as an excuse to check out some boys, when we finally arrived at a plain-faced storefront building. Startled, I glanced at Dawn, who flashed an encouraging smile and walked inside. I followed her then stopped short, captivated by a room of beautiful young Black men and women in black pants and powder blue shirts, many with black berets perched on their Afros. I wondered what alternate universe we had stepped into. Dawn was welcomed with hugs and smiles by two tall, thin young men with towering Afros and an air of authority. She introduced them as her cousins, the Dixon brothers. I stared, unable to form a coherent response.

"Hello, sister," the one with the green eyes said. The brown-eyed one smiled down at me, gestured towards a worn sofa, and invited us to have a seat.

Sister?

I plopped onto the sofa, breathless and giddy.

Those two syllables were the sweetest I'd heard in a long time. I felt embraced, welcomed and best of all, understood. In that moment, I realized how I'd started anticipating the eyeballs scanning me for ethnic clues, the queries about my background, the suspicions that I wasn't fully human beneath my clothes.

At first, I was overwhelmed by the Dixon brothers' good looks, but eventually my brain cleared enough to register Aaron as the older one, with brooding dark eyes and an intense, no-nonsense vibe. Elmer was the green-eyed one with the easy smile and exuberant charm. I later met their younger brother, Michael, who had a cute baby face and laid-back demeanor that made me feel instantly at home.

"What kind of place is this?" I asked Dawn, studying the young men and women moving through the storefront in a focused, disciplined manner, exuding a vibe of intense purpose.

"The Black Panther Party headquarters," she said.

Unsure what a Black Panther was, I struggled to take it all in. Sandbags lined the walls and some of the Panthers sat cleaning guns. I'd never been that close to weapons. My mind percolated with questions.

Soon, Elmer gathered a crowd in the front room, saying it was time for Political Education class. Class? I wondered if this was some kind of school. Posters and signs lined the walls, proclaiming the BLACK PANTHER PARTY FOR SELF-DEFENSE, SEATTLE CHAPTER. They handed us copies of the Black Panther newspaper, which included their Ten-Point Program, What We Want, What We Believe.

The list, simple and logical, called for equality in Black and all oppressed communities: the power to determine their destiny; full employment; an end to capitalist robberies; decent housing, fit for human shelter; decent education that taught true history; free health care; an immediate end to police brutality and murder, and to all wars of aggression; freedom for all those held in government and military prisons and jails; trials with peer juries; and land, bread, housing, education, clothing, justice, peace and community control of modern technology.

The Political Education discussion focused on the Black Panther Party serving the community with free food and health care. The Panthers broke down oppression and inequality along economic, not racial, lines. They explained the inherent class inequities of capitalism in a way that put the world around me into clear perspective. The conversations showed how racial and ethnic differences had been used to pit people in different groups against each other.

Every time we visited, the Panthers were polite, respectful and taking care of Party business. They prepared the newspapers for sale, bagged groceries for needy families and conducted Political Education classes. I was outraged when they told us how the police were plotting to attack and even murder Party members in various cities, including Seattle. While the Panthers quietly cleaned and checked their weapons, Aaron assured us that the guns were strictly for self-defense in case the police attacked.

I soon realized what was so different about the Dixon brothers and the other young men in the Party: none had the predatory vibe so common with the guys in our school and neighborhood. Their eyes didn't skate around our blooming curves, their lips didn't beckon us to "come get some of this, girl," then curse us as we scurried away in terror. They treated us like equals with brains. I basked in the relief of it all in as the calendar rolled towards Labor Day and the start of ninth grade. This was so much better than school. This was life!

I didn't know at the time, but Aaron was college-aged, and Elmer and Michael were still in high school. We watched them plan and build the Carolyn

Downs Medical Clinic, named after a young, beautiful Panther woman who had passed away. We witnessed them create a thriving Free Breakfast program that fed hundreds of children each weekday. It didn't seem extraordinary when they raised awareness about sickle cell anemia and provided testing for the condition, or when they filled grocery bags with donated food they'd gathered to feed families in need. I was mesmerized by their discipline and dedication to the community.

The Dixon brothers and the Panther Party were good for my shaky confidence. They treated me like I was intelligent, capable and caring. Inspired by their example of grassroots activism through service, I felt a growing sense of purpose and the power of being part of a cause.

On our last visit before school started, the vibe in the Panther house was changed. The Panthers were tight-lipped, eyes wary, speaking tersely. The stack of sandbags grew higher and the stash of guns and ammunition ballooned. Elmer put a hand on each of our shoulders and explained that we'd need to stay away from headquarters for a while. "Things are heating up with the pigs," he said. "Comrades are getting gunned down, and we wouldn't want anything to happen to you."

"Right on," Dawn and I said in unison, exchanging sad glances.

Tears sprung to my eyes at the thought of harm coming to the Panthers and of being shut out of this inspiring sanctuary. I was in a funk for days, angry at the police for threatening young people who were working so hard to help others.

Just when I thought things couldn't get worse, Mom said she'd signed me up for some new thing called the "Voluntary Racial Transfer Program," where I'd be shipped to the north end of Seattle to attend some school called Jane Addams.

"I don't know anybody at Jane Addams!"

"Oh, but you do. That's where Linda goes to school."

The mention of Linda's name meant it was a done deal. Linda Steinmann had been one of my closest friends since preschool, where we bonded over our mutual love of Alvin and the Chipmunks. Our sisterhood was cemented when we were skipped together from kindergarten to first grade at age five. Linda had long, chestnut brown hair, bright blue eyes, and a knack for seeing into the heart of any person or situation with startling clarity.

We'd gone through preschool and elementary school side by side. Since

Linda's mom was divorced like mine, and her younger sister was the same age as Greg, they generously let us share their after-school babysitter at Linda's house. In many ways, we felt like family.

She was also White, but for some reason, I didn't feel the need to keep up my guard around her. We kind of lost touch after she moved to the north end and we attended different middle schools on the opposite sides of town. I loved Linda like a sister, but I couldn't imagine invading her territory any more than I could picture her suddenly turning up at Meany.

When I asked why I had to be racially transferred, Mom answered that it was to integrate the schools. I rolled my eyes and countered that I was already naturally integrated. Mom nailed me with The Look, signaling that further resistance was futile and the conversation had ended.

I finished my dinner in silence, wondering how life could get any worse. I'd finally learned how things worked at Meany, finding my place in a multi-colored environment after navigating a mostly White elementary school. I wasn't ready to start anew surrounded by strangers in foreign territory.

In desperation, I called upon the spirit of Malcolm X, summoned the courage of the Dixon brothers, and resigned myself to a year of misery.

The 1900 Census

Racial categories for the 1900 census were nearly the same as those in 1880: W for White, B for Black (Negro or of Negro descent), Ch for Chinese, Jp for Japanese, and In for Indian.

This census dropped the term "Mulatto" and was the first to use "Negro or Negro descent" for Black people. And in an attempt to identify the tribal affiliations of Native Americans, enumerators were told to write "zero" if the Indian had no White blood, and to write either one-half, one-quarter, one-eighth, or other fractions of White blood. They also tried to distinguish Native Americans who were from Canada, Mexico, and the United States by asking their country of birth.

The 1910 Census

A permanent Bureau of the Census was formed in 1902, so this was the first census conducted under this new agency. Most racial categories stayed the same, but the government went back to trying to measure Black blood. "Enumerators were instructed to assign the letter B only to those individuals whom they considered to be full-blooded Negroes, while the term Mulatto indicated all other persons having some proportion or perceptible trace of Negro blood."

This census also had an "Other race" for people who the enumerators couldn't identify as White, Black, Mulatto, Chinese, Japanese, or Indian. "Ot" for Other was written on the left margins of the form.

My paternal grandfather, Vernon Warmass Stone, age 17, was listed in the 1910 census with his family in Des Moines, Iowa. His mother, Izeaial Robinson, was 42; his stepfather, Armstead Robinson, was 45. Vernon's brothers Lamar and Ceciel were 15 and 14, respectively. They were all assigned the racial designation of M for Mulatto.

The 1920 Census

The racial categories for the 1920 census were the same as those in 1910.

Rosalyn Weisberg Stone, 1940s

Chapter 9: The Wheels on the Bus

The dreaded first day of ninth grade arrived. Instead of walking up the hill to school, I took a few steps to the city bus stop in front of our house. The big yellow school bus pulled up and farted to a stop. I climbed aboard and sat alone, scrunching low in my seat to glare out the window.

Our bus supervisor was a short, round woman with a light brown face, a friendly smile, and rules that went on for days. The other kids had been bussed together for seventh and eighth grades, so they knew each other well. I'd never felt more alone.

After riding for what felt like an hour through strange streets, we pulled up to Jane Addams to see groups of White students staring at our bus like it was a spaceship about to dispense alien creatures. Inside the building, I desperately searched for Linda in the sea of faces.

Linda had been my anchor through elementary school, coolly intelligent with a warm heart. Even though she was the smartest girl in any class, she never acted that way. It's just that whatever came out of her mouth usually made more sense than anyone else's, sometimes even the teachers.

My habit of mentally cataloguing people by race helped to maintain order in my multicolored world. From kindergarten through fourth grade, I worked hard to keep my worlds separate. Home was people and families of different colors. School was mostly White, with a light sprinkling of students from other cultures; Greg and I were the only Mixed kids. At home, I was relaxed, daring, and outgoing. At school, I was reserved, quiet, and masked. I chose each word carefully and guarded my feelings. My language at home was freer, more voluptuous and unbound. Switching between the codes and colors of each environment was second nature.

The other kids in our neighborhood went to nearby Stevens Elementary School. Greg and I went to Seward instead, because Mom didn't have a car and it was on the bus routes to her job at the gas company. I don't know what magic she worked to get permission for us to go to school beyond our neighborhood boundaries. But since we'd gone to preschool and elementary school with the same kids, Seward was familiar and comfortable. There were maybe three or four Black kids, a few Asians and a pair of Mexican sisters.

On the first day of the fifth grade, my convenient little coping system was shattered. A bus pulled up to dispense a crowd of Black students, strangers. I heard these new students came from Horace Mann, an elementary school in the Central Area, because their school building was being renovated.

I watched them from a distance, not quite ready to step out of my reserved school persona to relate to the new energies they brought into the environment. I waited to see how they'd read me. Or whether they'd notice me at all.

It wasn't long before their eyes sought me out. They always spoke, letting me know they'd pegged me without making a big deal about it.

Until James Brown.

For some reason, these newcomers had gathered in the cafeteria to play music and dance, just like we did at home. The other students crowded around to gawk at the Black kids jamming to the irresistible funk of Papa James Brown singing "I Feel Good."

I watched warily, my foot tapping. I stood rigid, next to Linda who looked from me to the dancers and back again. I felt the twinge of conflicting personas. Then the tallest girl with the wide smile who was in my class, caught my eye and waved me over.

I walked awkwardly into the circle, glancing back at Linda's bewildered face. The Black kids wanted to see how down I was. The kids I went to school with my whole life stared at me, mouths open.

My movements were stiff at first. I closed my eyes to shut out the stares, and let the music seep past my school mask and armor. My body loosened … and hit the beat.

I opened my eyes to see the Black kids nodding and smiling at me. I felt the weight of moving between two worlds melt away until the song faded and the communal dance wound down. I knew that I'd been publicly claimed.

"I didn't know you could do that," Linda said as we left the cafeteria. I sensed the first rip in the seam of our friendship, but didn't know what to do about it. I felt guilty for going where she couldn't join me, but enjoyed the strange pleasure of being able to feel like myself at school for the very first time.

Four years later, as an invader on Linda's turf in Jane Addams, we were pushed even further apart. Missing our friendship, I tried to get her attention, hoping that we could bridge our worlds, maybe meet in the middle. But our rhythms seemed too discordant. Here, she knew the beats, the codes, and the moves. Addams was her music, her truth and her tribe. I couldn't see an easy point of entry, or common ground for us to meet. This made the Siberian wasteland of Jane Addams Middle School feel even more forlorn.

I missed Meany, longing for Dawn and even stupid Green Eyes. I missed the girls trippin' over my hair in the bathroom, the dozens, the sharp bursts of laughter, the music of color and the color of music in everyday chit-chat.

The super-whiteness of Jane Addams wasn't just in the complexions of its native population, but in the way the teachers studied you extra hard, like they weren't sure what to do with you. Or the way the students hurried through the hallways, their eyes studiously averted. Sometimes if the girls caught you looking at them, they'd flick a tight-lipped smile that disappeared so quickly you thought you'd imagined it. The atmosphere was frosty, the language stern and clipped, the faces sometimes curious, often closed. Seattle hadn't experienced all-out Jim Crow segregation, but there was nothing warm or welcoming about this place. And there were no signs that anyone was interested in "integrating" anything.

Chapter 10: "Let My People Go!"

Since most of the Black kids at Jane Addams were bused in, I was surprised to learn that a few Black students actually lived in that school district. I made friends with a girl who was in some of my classes. She was brown-skinned and the kind of cute that would blossom into high-cheekboned beauty as she grew older. Like me, she had a few pimples and a couple extra pounds. As we got to know each other, I was stunned to learn that she'd grown up way out in that neighborhood. That seemed even crazier than being forced to ride a bus across town.

"Where do you live?" she asked me.

"In the Central Area, like the other kids who are bussed."

"What are you?"

"Mixed."

"Like with what?" She talked like the White kids at Addams.

"Black and Jewish."

"But you can't be Black and Jewish at the same time," she insisted. "Those two things just don't go together!" She jumped up, startling me.

"Black people are Christian and go to church. Jewish people are Jewish and go to—"

"Synagogue," I said with a sigh.

"Yeah, see what I mean?" she said. "They don't fit together! So, you can't be both."

I stared at her, wondering if growing up Black in such a White environment had damaged her brain. I thought about it. If none of the Black people she'd seen were Jewish, and none of the Jewish people were Black, maybe it was hard for her to imagine one person being both. But I was a living, breathing example that it was possible. That's when I realized that the only people I knew who were Black and Jewish were my brother, Greg, and myself. We knew lots of other Mixed kids, but nobody else who was our specific combination.

I brushed away the rush of sadness at that revelation and stood to face her. "I can be Black and Jewish because that's what I am," I said slowly through clenched teeth. "Okay?"

"You mean like Sammy Davis, Jr.?"

"Hell no! Sammy Davis Jr. isn't—well, he's different, that's all. But we're both real. If you don't believe that, you can't be my friend."

She stared at me for a long minute, then nodded one time.

And we never discussed my identity again.

That conversation reminded me why I'd dropped out of Hebrew School.

There wasn't much in our world that was specifically Jewish. Mom wove Yiddish words and phrases into everyday conversation, and took us to Brenner Brothers Bakery deep in the Central Area for bagels, pumpernickel and the like. While the part of town we lived in had been predominantly Jewish before it became mostly Black, we weren't close enough to any Jewish classmates to talk on the phone or visit each other's homes.

The most Jewish flavor in our lives came from Mom's lifelong friend Molly, who lived in Portland, Oregon, with her three sons. On our occasional visits with them, we had formal Shabbat dinners on Friday night, complete with prayers in Hebrew and the rhythms of slightly familiar traditions.

When we visited Mom's family in Minneapolis, the Jewish vibe seemed more about the food and the culture than the actual religion. There were no formal rituals, and I never heard anybody mention going to synagogue.

When I was ten, Mom decided that Greg and I needed to learn some Jewish history and culture by spending Saturdays in Hebrew School. The quest for balance to the Blackness of our environment made sense to me.

While I didn't stand out physically among the Jewish kids, many of whom had dark hair (often curlier than mine) and what were called "olive" complexions, I was aware that I didn't fully fit in either. Nobody singled me out, asked what I was, or challenged my right to be there. But I knew, even if my peers didn't, of the fundamental differences between us.

I liked the way the teachers imparted the stories in the Torah to convey pride in being Jewish, against the backdrop of all the persecution our people had survived. I enjoyed our infrequent visits to the synagogue—the serene atmosphere and rituals that spoke of something ancient and enduring. But what I loved most was learning the Hebrew language, with its rich guttural tones and musical rumblings. I learned quickly, reading the entire Torah in Hebrew, and was disappointed when we hadn't advanced to the next level in the second year.

That was the year we read *The Diary of A Young Girl* by Anne Frank in my regular school. I felt every word, and identified with everything she described. I marveled at how her story made the unspeakable horrors of the Nazi Holocaust feel so immediate and so real. I waited for the teachers to require us to read about what Black people, and Native American people, had endured in this country. I was frustrated that they were so focused on what happened in Germany years earlier, but didn't seem to care about what had gone on—and was still going on—within our own borders.

Mom never pushed anything religious on us, but she agreed when I asked to add Hebrew prayers to our family meals, or hold a Seder for Passover. I knew that if I planned to have my Bat Mitzvah when I turned 13, I'd have to start serious preparation and studies soon. But I didn't know how much of the other parts of myself I'd have to give up for that kind of formal commitment.

Fate and a bathtub full of nastiness intervened before I had to make that choice. My father lived a few blocks from the synagogue. When Mom had to work on Saturdays, Greg and I walked to his house after Hebrew School.

One Saturday as I stood outside the synagogue waiting for Greg's class to end, I heard a group of neighborhood friends calling my name from across the busy street. "Hey, Terri!"

"Hey!" I waved to them.

"What are you doing over there?" one of the girls shouted, squinting at the Jewish kids standing around me.

As I was figuring out how to explain Hebrew School to my friends, a boy from Hebrew School tapped my shoulder. "How do you know those schvartzes?"

"Don't call them that! They're my friends. And I'm--"

"Are you gonna come with us?" The girls' voices carried over the cars zooming down the hill between us.

"Which side are you on, anyway?" the boy asked, looking from my friends to me.

"I can't!" I hollered across to my friends. "I have to go to my Dad's."

With a final wave, they went on their way.

"Well?" he pressed. "Have you made up your mind?"

At that moment, I felt like the rope in a tug-of-war, with both teams pulling to get me on their side of the line. "There's nothing to decide, Randy. I'm both."

"I thought you were one of us," he interrupted, shooting me a look of disgust as he walked over to a group of our classmates. He whispered to them, then pointed at me, shaking his head. They stared as if really seeing me for the first time. I didn't think this was part of the Jewish history and culture that Mom intended for me to learn.

Greg came out of the synagogue, and we headed to Dad's house. "What's wrong with you?" he asked. I shrugged, too upset to speak. When we arrived, Dad was drinking as usual. He didn't normally give us chores but this must have been a special day because as soon as we walked in, he pulled me aside and informed me that I had to wash a mess of chitlins. Since we were practically strangers, it was no surprise that he didn't know how much I hated the slimy pig guts.

He'd taught Mom how to cook soul food, including chitlins, when they'd been together. She still made them sometimes, but she never asked me to help clean them. I never forgot my first taste of the so-called delicacy as a toddler. No matter how much I chewed, my throat closed up so I couldn't swallow them. I was too young to understand what intestines were, but my body was adamant that none of that mess would be allowed to enter my tender young system.

Dad led me to a bathtub halfway filled with the nauseating pile of hog guts. I tried to back out, but he grabbed my arm. "You know how to clean 'em?" he asked with a smirk. I shook my head, trying not to gag. He showed me what to do, then left me there while he went out to drink and laugh with his wife and friends.

I half-heartedly cleaned some of them, seasoning the gross slime with my angry tears. I kept hearing the Jewish boy's voice calling my friends that word, schvartze. I knew it was the Yiddish version of nigger; I knew the hate it conveyed and the weight that it carried. Between the chitlins, schvartze, and the horrible feeling that I had to explain myself to both sides, I'd reached a breaking point.

As soon as Mom's car rolled up, I jumped in and announced that I was through with Hebrew School. I guess the look on my face was enough, because she didn't ask why.

I was angry and frustrated at Randy's pressure to choose a side and at my new school friend's insistence that Black and Jewish didn't belong together. What made them think they knew more about my identity than I did?

The year before, I had my first introduction to Black Christian worship when I'd visited Dawn's church. I compared the bright splashes of color, high-voltage singing, sermons and nonstop movement of Dawn's church with the cool decor, soft music, and soothing prayers of the synagogue. I'd been shocked when the Christian choir burst into singing "Let My People Go," a song I knew from the synagogue and associated only with Jews. I hadn't known that it was a traditional Negro spiritual where Black people coded their longing for freedom in the struggles of the Jewish people long before.

As the choir's harmonic voices soared, I saw parallels between Black and Jewish struggles for freedom and justice. It was jarring to feel the different parts of me—always so disparate and requiring such a delicate balancing act—collide in a single song. For a few brief minutes, I felt the strands of my ancestry knitting together. I hugged the feeling close, wanting it to last as long as possible.

My new friend's insistence that I "couldn't be" the things that I was reminded me how powerful that brief feeling had been and how rare it was in my life.

Chapter 11: You Can Be...

My father's attitude about my identity made me wonder if he regretted having made Mixed children. I couldn't tell if he hated his own Blackness or thought I'd be better off pretending that it didn't exist.

Though he lived nearby, he stayed on the outskirts of our lives. While Mom did double-duty as a parent, he made it clear that he had no interest in playing a fatherly role. He didn't know what we liked to eat, that I was a bookworm, tomboy, and aspiring author, or that Greg was both a natural salesperson who could convince anyone to do anything and a gifted athlete who taught me to swim underwater when he was only three. And Dad never paid a dime of the ridiculously paltry ten dollars a month that the court assigned him as child support for Greg and me.

Though she deserved that money and much more, Mom never complained about Dad's lack of financial support. She didn't say much about him at all, except that he'd been the love of her life—handsome, witty, charismatic, and talented. As a young tap dancer, his style was compared to his idols, the Nicholas Brothers. When Dad's knees gave out from his acrobatic dance feats, he channeled his rhythms into his hands to become a jazz drummer. And though he'd been an alcoholic all his life, he was disciplined. He never got drunk during the workweek or drove a car while under the influence. I'd never seen or heard evidence of his musical talents, so I had to take Mom's word for it. I was two years old when he left and after that, we never exchanged a smile, a hug, or a tender moment. I never heard him say, "I love you," or "I'm glad you're my kid." The wit, talent, and charisma that Mom described seemed buried in a haze of alcohol and bitterness.

On special occasions, Dad invited Greg and me over for his delicious barbecue. On regular weekend visits when he wasn't on the grill, he listened to good jazz, drank beer, drenched his food in hot sauce and got on my nerves. But as his child, part of me still hungered to forge a bond with him, find common ground, a way to make sense of our connection.

One Saturday after the chitlin-washing disaster, we sat in his house watching news reports of the race riots blazing across American's inner cities, with cries of "Black Power " coming from the screen. He stared impassively, nursing a beer. Desperate to forge a sense of connection with him, I gathered my nerve and reached out to share something close to my heart.

"I read this book by Malcolm X—"

He set his beer bottle down hard on the wooden coffee table. "I don't need to read about that shit. I've lived it." He studied my face as though he'd never seen it before. "What's your problem? Why are you trying so hard to be Black?"

"I'm not trying to be anything," I retorted. "Why are you trying to deny your Blackness?"

We locked eyes.

"Stop telling people you're Black. You can be—" he waved his free arm around— "anything you want. The way you look, you can tell people anything."

"I don't need to tell people I'm 'anything' when I'm already something!" I said, my voice rising with frustration.

He looked sad. "You're too young to understand what you're throwing away."

"Throwing away?" I cried. "I'll bet you haven't even heard of the Black Panther Party for Self-Defense!"

He snorted. "Those young spooks don't know what they're doing. The ofays are gonna kill them all."

"At least they're proud of who they are!"

He shook his head. "Yelling 'Black Power' won't get anyone anywhere. You need to stop holding yourself back with that shit." He changed the channel from the news of racial unrest to a game show.

I ran outside to sit on his porch in the rain, crying nonstop until Mom picked us up. That night, I laid awake asking God why George Kelly Stone had to be my father, why the man who gave me my blackness was telling me to throw it away, deny it, because he believed that living a lie was a better option.

I had flashes of memory from when he'd lived with us before Greg was born. As a toddler, I watched adoringly as he shaved in the bathroom mirror. I sat on his lap while we watched "Gunsmoke" and "Bonanza" on our black-and-white TV. Sometimes he gave me a sip from the foam at the top of his beer, back when he drank it out of a tall glass. I hated the taste, but loved the feeling of being close to him. Of being a daughter. Of having a daddy.

On the flip side, I remembered him and Mom shouting at each other in what felt like an endless loop of conflicts about money and other women. I was two years old and Greg was in Mom's womb when she finally put him out. I vividly recalled how the tension in the house went with him. I didn't understand what was happening, didn't have the words to explain it to myself, but that sensation of blessed calm after the storm was branded onto my soul.

I didn't hate him for leaving Mom, but I hated how he'd hurt her. And for all the times he'd said he was coming to see Greg and me but didn't show up. Countless Saturday mornings when I dressed up, hyped on hope, staring out the window for hours in search of a car that never came. I didn't know then that he was a responsible alcoholic—drinking heavily from Friday night through Sunday—not wanting to drive while under the influence. With "weekend visitation rights," he might have saved our lives by not putting us in his car. Back then, as a young child, all I knew was the wrenching pain of abandonment. My young mind reasoned that he stayed away because I wasn't good enough.

I recalled one of the rare times he had shown up and taken us with him to the Madison Plaza Drugstore on 23rd and Madison. I was eight and Greg was five. We were about to go into the store when a long-faced Black man in a hat called, "Hey, Kelly!"

Dad smiled and motioned the man over. "Hey, man, how you doin'?" They slapped palms as the stranger stared hard at Greg and me, eyes full of questions I was already starting to recognize.

"That you?" he asked, nodding his head in our direction.

"Yeah, man," Dad said with a self-conscious chuckle. "Ain't they pretty?"

I knew what "pretty" meant. Dad was bragging about having fathered kids with real light skin and wavy hair. I stared down at his spit-shined black Stacy Adams shoes, swallowing the lump of fire that rose in my throat. That's all we were to him: trophies in some one-up game that grown-ups liked to play.

I wondered whether Dad would view or treat us differently if we shared his coppery color. Would he brag about our looks then?

When he claimed I "could be anything," I heard him suggesting he'd be cool with me changing my name, denying my ancestors, lying about every aspect of my being, and pretending he didn't even exist. He acted like Blackness was only for those whose bodies didn't give them other options, a "stain" that I should avoid and escape for as long as I could pull it off.

At the dawn of my teen years, as our nation rocked and rolled with shifting race relations, what I wanted most was for Dad to hold up his end of the deal as the parent of Mixed kids by standing tall and being proud of his identity, like Mom was proud of hers. Even if he hadn't wanted Greg and me, even if he didn't love us, or felt something but didn't know how to show it, the very least he could do was express pride in his own ancestry. It was hard to respect him when he wouldn't give me that.

Chapter 12: In a Strange Land

"You know why White girls are better than Black girls?" one of the boys on the school bus asked loudly.

My head snapped up from my book, and the air tightened around me. A few girls argued, then other boys joined in. "White girls are better because they're not as much trouble. And they do what you want with no back talk."

"Yeah," another boy piped up in a squeaky voice. "They know how to let a man be a man."

The circle of boys kept making their claims as the girls accused them of disrespecting their mothers, sisters, grandmas, aunties and cousins.

Just when it looked like fists were about to fly, the bus supervisor walked up on them, her usually soft voice at no-nonsense decibel. "Stop this foolishness right now," she demanded. The sparring students glared at each other across the aisle, their argument deflating under her stern gaze.

I knew that refrain like the chorus of a hit song. Some of the Black boys in my neighborhood often went out of their way to inform us--Black girls and Mixed girls alike—why we weren't as good as White girls, listing the same reasons the boys on the bus had given. I wondered where they'd learned this, what made them think this way, why they were so quick to put down their own in favor of White girls. This was less than two years after Jim Crow laws had been struck down, and it hadn't been that long since Black boys and men were lynched for even being suspected or accused of looking at or speaking to a White woman.

I wondered if any of the boys from the bus were trying to mack on the White girls at Addams. Maybe they were just captivated by the idea of White female flesh as "forbidden fruit." Or maybe they truly believed that White girls were superior. The whole thing made my head pound.

Maybe that's why I said "yes" when Ray asked me to "go with him." Ray was a soft-spoken, medium brown, polite boy from Texas who lived down in the valley near Mamie and Uncle Ernie. While my main thoughts of romance were informed by the syrupy songs pouring from my radio, and Ray's presence didn't make me tingle, he didn't offend or repel me either. So just like that, I had my first official boyfriend.

He went to another school so we talked on the phone during the week and saw each other on weekends. After a couple of dry-lipped smooches, he tried to introduce me to French kissing. The first few times I jumped back, wiping the wet from my upper lip, unsure of the rules. I wanted to feel the way Aretha sounded when she sang "You Make Me Feel Like A Natural Woman" -- heart filled with a yearning conjured from sweet beats, seductive melodies, and promises of paradise. Little by little, I acquiesced, still not sure what all the fuss was about. I kept waiting for my new beau to tell me why White girls were better. But he never did. So, we exchanged wallet-sized school photos, writing sweet messages and "xoxo" on the back.

One boy at Jane Addams was actually friendly to me. Tim was tall, thin and freckled, with straight brown hair hanging into his big, brown Paul McCartney eyes. He sat across from me in history class. If we got to our seats early, he'd make me laugh with corny jokes about the teacher. And he had lots of questions about where I lived. I answered patiently, figuring he'd never been outside of Seattle's north end.

Even with Tim's friendly chatter, Jane Addams was still frigid. At lunch, most of us bus kids huddled together in the cafeteria, enjoying a brief moment of letting down our armor to exhale and recharge before venturing back into the pale icy world of voluntary racial transfers.

As usual, a book helped me understand and define my predicament. I read Stranger in a Strange Land by Robert Heinlein, a popular science fiction novel about a man who grows up on Mars, then comes to Earth where he struggles to adapt to humans and their ways. I identified with his journey, wondering what part of this unyielding school would ever hold a comfortable place for me.

Vernon Warness Stone, my Paternal Grandfather, a barber.

Chapter 13: Say It Loud!

The "Black is Beautiful" movement was in full bloom in the fall of 1968. Afros were ubiquitous, the Afro picks and metal cake cutters used to style them were jammed into back pockets or bouncing in the hair itself. Dashikis blossomed in bright colors, and young people proudly flaunted their burgeoning racial consciousness.

Some older Black people like Dad considered the word Black a slur. They'd lived through being called Colored and Negro, and weren't always on board with this bold new assertion of pride.

I was impressed and inspired when U.S. Olympic track stars Tommie Smith and John Carlos saluted Black Power during the 1968 Summer Olympic games in Mexico City, Mexico. On their way to the podium to receive their gold and bronze medals respectively, they removed their shoes to protest poverty as they strode toward the podium. They each wore beads and a scarf to protest the lynchings of Black men, women and children. And when the U.S. national anthem blared, they lowered their heads and raised black-gloved fists high into the air. The world stopped in its tracks and took notice.

A popular saying in the streets was that "Blackness is a state of mind." Songs about protest, pride and revolution were interspersed among the love jams on the radio. Then the Black Power movement got an official anthem.

Just weeks after I thought I'd perish in the icy loneliness of Jane Addams, Celia rushed over to my house to share a new 45 record with me. We listened to it on the pink-and-white record player in my bedroom, mesmerized by James Brown commanding us to "Say It Loud! I'm Black and I'm Proud!"

A chorus of children's voices echoed the proud cry. The heart-pumping anthem felt raw and dangerous, a brash strike in the face of racism and police brutality. Celia demonstrated the dance to go with the song, hips pushed to the side, arms thrust high. I borrowed her record to practice in the mirror.

Studying my image while mouthing the in-your-face lyrics, I wondered how Black I had to be to affirm that level of Black pride aloud. Was half enough? What if I was required to prove my qualifications?

I was Black enough to be bussed across town to integrate into a White school.

Celia shouted the slogan with ease. I tried to join her, but the words caught in my throat. Instead, I let my hips, hands and feet speak for me. I pondered the continuing mysteries of light-and dark-skinned dynamics. Considered the baffling ways that some people responded to my hair.

I silently mouthed the lyrics as my body joined the call-and-response.

While it wasn't clear just how much Black pride I was entitled to holler to the skies, Papa JB spoke to my heart and fortified my young soul. In the moment, that felt like nearly enough.

One day the tall, freckled boy named Tim in history class asked point blank, "Why'd you come to Addams anyway?"

"To racially integrate your school."

"But you don't look Black." he said accusingly.

"I'm Black enough to get bussed out here."

"How does it work? If your dad is Black, you're Black?"

"That's dumb," I laughed. The only rule I knew was the one Mom had taught me: that you're considered Jewish if your mother is Jewish because you grew in her body. The rules about Blackness didn't seem nearly as simple or universal. Blackness is a state of mind.

"Which boys are better—White ones or Black ones?" Tim asked. I flashed to the Black boys who preferred White girls, and Dawn demanding to know the color of my future husband the year before.

"No such thing as 'better,'" I said. "This is who I go with." I reached into my purse for my wallet, and showed him Ray's photo.

"You like that baboon?"

My brain stalled at my "friend's" swift change in attitude. I snatched

Ray's picture back and jammed it into my purse.

I avoided Tim for a few days. When I caught him staring at me in class, I gave him my dirtiest look and turned away.

Back in the neighborhood, Ray had worked up to a proper French kiss. While I didn't pull away or want to gag anymore, it still didn't feel like a love song. It wasn't nasty, just strange. The more we kissed, the further Ray wanted to go. We didn't talk much. I didn't know if he loved books the way I did, or hosted characters and voices in his head that quieted only when they were transferred to paper. But he wasn't nasty, and he kept walking up the hills to see me. The boyfriend thing wasn't too bad. At least it took my mind off of school.

Sometimes when I walked through the halls of Jane Addams, James Brown's words looped through my mind like a secret password. One day, I bopped into history class on that bold beat. Tim greeted me with a smile. "How's your boyfriend?"

I turned away, hands clenching and unclenching.

"Don't be mad, okay?" His voice was soft, wheedling. His freckles stood out, shades lighter than his innocent-looking brown eyes.

"What do you want?"

"For you not to have a boyfriend."

I rolled my eyes and went to my seat. Was this how White guys macked on you? At the closing bell, I hurried out. Tim caught up. "Can I walk you to class?"

I shrugged, careful to keep my distance. After a few steps, he moved closer, bumping my hip with his. I stared ahead, unsure what to expect.

"Check this out," he said.

"I can't be late," I said, looking around for an adult.

"C'mon, it'll just take a minute."

Before I could respond, Tim grabbed my arm, pulled me around a corner and backed me against a locker. "Can your gorilla boyfriend do this?" he asked, mashing his mouth into mine, his tongue probing my lips like an angry snake.

"Quit!" I pushed him away, mesmerized by the mottled red of his face, his beautiful brown eyes shooting pure hatred at me.

"I knew it! You only like Black apes, don't you?"

"What?" I wiped my mouth hard on the back of my hand. "Get off me!"

"I don't have to, you dirty nigger!" he spat.

The word sucked the breath from my body. The class bell rang but I was paralyzed. I wanted to devastate Tim with the worst word I could think of. "You punk-ass Nazi mu-tha-fuck-a," I growled. I'd heard and thought and even felt that word, but never spoken it aloud. I made sure to draw it out and hit the downbeat extra hard. Tim and I were locked in a death-stare until I turned and somehow made it to my next class.

The teacher started to ask why I was late, but I just stomped to my desk and sat down with a thud. I wanted every movement to trumpet my rage. I wanted to hurt somebody, I didn't care who. I didn't hear a thing the teacher said, my mind consumed with "dirty nigger" on repeat. Felt Tim's invading mouth and tongue, his hands bruising my shoulders, his eyes shooting arrows of superiority into my soul.

I fantasized about calling the Dixon brothers and the Black Panther Party to march into Jane Addams and teach Tim a lesson. I'd heard how they'd saved women from abusive partners and prostitutes from their pimps. I wanted them to stride into this field of White smugness with their black jackets, turtlenecks and berets, holding their rifles aloft and defending the race. Defending me.

On the bus home, I stared out the window, avoiding everyone. "Why you look so mad?" one of the boys asked. I shook my head, afraid I'd start crying. He sat next to me. "What happened?" He was big for his age with a deep, mannish voice. He'd always been nice to me.

"Tim. This White boy—" I could barely eke out a whisper.

"That tall, skinny one with the freckles?" he asked.

I nodded. "He…" I gulped the air. "He called me…" I was losing my battle at fighting back tears.

"He called you that?" he asked gruffly.

I nodded, wiping my face with both hands.

My brother, Gregory, and me

"You swear 'fore God it was him?"

"Yeah," I gasped, raising my right hand.

I couldn't sleep that night, my brain locked in endless loops of rage and frustration. I wanted to smash Tim's face into a bloody pulp. I felt sick that I had no one to call for help. I longed to tell Mom, but I didn't want to yank her out of her "people are just people" idealism to grapple with the ugliness of my world. She worked too hard, gave too much to Greg and me, for me not to try to buffer her from the pain. Besides, she'd sentenced me to that icy hell thinking it would improve me. I knew how much she hated that cruel, demeaning word; I couldn't tell her that I'd been slimed with its power, and obsessed with the things it made me want to do.

On the bus the next morning, the same boy motioned for me to sit next to him. "Remember, don't say anything to anybody," he warned.

"Swear to God," I promised.

All day I felt exhausted but hyped. I didn't search for Linda. I avoided looking at any White person. I didn't pretend to listen to any of my teachers. No matter how many words I scribbled in the margins of my schoolwork, I couldn't come up with a single one that had the power of "nigger." Tim beat me with a weapon he knew I couldn't match. It was the nuclear bomb of slurs, leaving ruin and devastation in its wake. The worst part was not having any effective way to fight back.

Later, I heard a rumor that somebody had slammed Tim's head into a metal radiator in a school hallway. I wondered if the boy on the bus had done it and prayed that if he had, he wouldn't get caught or punished. It comforted me to think that Tim might have suffered some pain.

I didn't see Tim for a few weeks. When I finally did, he refused to look my way. I missed the talks we'd had before he showed his true colors. I missed his warm eyes and easy grin. How could I have known what lurked behind them? Sick with shame, I vowed never to let my guard down or be that stupid again.

I didn't tell anybody about it, not even Greg. I daydreamed about ditching the "Voluntary Racial Transfer Program" to hang out at the Black Panther Party headquarters where my nascent rage could be put to good use. Instead, I rode to and from Siberia for hours every week, disappearing into invisibility and impotence until I returned to the sanctuary of home.

The 1930 Census

The 1930 census expanded to ten racial categories: Mexican, Filipino, Hindu, and Korean were added to White, Negro, Indian, Chinese, Japanese, and Other. This was also the first census to use the one-drop, or hypo-descent rule, to count Black people:

A person of mixed White and Negro blood was to be returned as Negro, no matter how small the percentage of Negro blood; someone part Indian and part Negro also was to be listed as Negro unless the Indian blood predominated and the person was generally accepted as an Indian in the community. A person of mixed White and Indian blood was to be returned as an Indian, except where the percentage of Indian blood was very small, or where he or she was regarded as White in the community.

Any mixture of "White" and some "Other race" was reported according to the race of the parent who was not White. Mixtures of colored races other than Black were listed according to the father's race.

The Filipino category was added to record the growing number who immigrated to the U.S. as laborers, most working in agriculture and domestic service.

My mother's family, the Weisbergs, was listed in this census as living on Oliver Avenue North in Minneapolis. Her parents were in their thirties, and she was six years old.

The 1940 Census

In 1940, the general racial categories remained the same as in 1930, except that Mexicans were listed as White unless they could be identified as Indians or as a race other than White. "Other races" had to specify the person's lineage. Prior to this census, Eskimos and Aleuts were included in the Indian category, but this census counted them separately in Alaska.

In this census, my mother Rosalyn's family had moved to Sixth Avenue North. My father, Kelly, his first wife, Kathryn (nicknamed Katie), and their daughter Shirley, lived nearby on Fourth Avenue North. Mom was sixteen and Dad was twenty-three. I don't know whether their paths ever crossed during this time.

Chapter 14: Best of Both What?

Ninth grade was barely over before Mom dropped an even worse bomb: Apparently isolating me to Siberia for a school year hadn't produced the desired results. She signed me up for three more years of the "Voluntary Racial Transfer" program at Roosevelt High School in the north end. I gave up any hope of ever enjoying school again.

I was afraid that Mom was sending me across town to make me into a White girl. While she disapproved of people who passed and I wasn't sure if she shared Dad's conviction that I "could be anything," I couldn't help but suspect her motives.

A few weeks later, I overheard her talking with Auntie Shirley on the phone about how I was "overcompensating by acting so Black all the time." She said she couldn't understand why I didn't take advantage of "having the best of both worlds."

Mom was fond of saying that Greg and I had "the best of both worlds." I reasoned that was something she imagined about being Mixed, but it didn't make sense to me. Maybe she envisioned a magical buffet of race and culture that allowed us to pick and choose certain features according to our preferences. Like I could go to the Black section and take the rhythm but leave the blues; heap my plate with triumph but wave away the tribulations. Then move to the White section, where everything was locked up and guarded like precious jewelry so I could look but not touch. What could I ask for there? A scoop of privilege, a serving of entitlement, a side dish of advantage? As if prejudice, discrimination and inequality weren't weighing down sections of that imaginary buffet, and I had full access to the advantages and power in the White section.

As if my desire could overcome centuries of prejudice, discrimination and inequity to melt hatred and oppression by sheer force of will.

My mother was one of the smartest, most insightful people I knew. I respected her stubborn commitment to her "best of both worlds" theory, but it had no place in the reality that I was learning to navigate. I wasn't "trying to be" Black. It wasn't an affectation or an act. Not even she or my father—the people who'd created me—seemed able to accept me as I was. They were trying to cram me into their fantasies of what a perfect Mixed person should be. That made me angry and sad. Most of all, it made me determined to find my truth and live it, regardless of what they thought.

In that summer of 1969, Black identity was still evolving in response to the social movements of the time. Notions like "soul" and "state of mind" were often cited as qualifiers. Despite Mom's frustrations, I never felt like I had to try to "be" Black because Blackness had claimed me as far back as I could remember. The prevailing concept that "one drop of Black blood made you Black" reflected the slave masters' rules for protecting their property, and the realities of Jim Crow segregation that came later. But for me it also meant that even that mythical single drop carried the power of history, struggle, resistance, and triumph that could not be denied. And in the United States, there was no middle ground, imaginary or otherwise, between Black and White.

One thing being bussed to Jane Addams helped me to see clearly is how Whiteness is defined by exclusion. The White world was built on the premise of keeping everyone else out, while working to control them and the spaces they could enter. White people made the rules and built the systems to enforce those rules. They controlled the resources to bolster the rules they made and the laws they wrote. They determined the definitions of words and pronounced their interpretations the official version every time. They alone decided what we learned in schools, what made it into news reports on television and radio and in newspapers. They created the advertising to persuade us what to buy, and they policed our access to those things while profiting from our business. Their world was built to ensure their advantage, and their version of reality was all they considered to be valid.

Blackness was forged in response to oppression. It was strong and fluid, able to adapt while retaining its essence. Unlike Whiteness, Blackness was by nature flexible--welcoming and inclusive--and Mixed identity was grounded in its proximity or response to that Blackness. If I was part of the spectrum of Blackness, it lived in my spirit and my heart, not through any effort on my part, but as a gift from my Ancestors. I hated that my parents didn't seem to understand this simple truth.

The contentious nature of race relations in the USA was even reflected in the race to conquer outer space. In the middle of summer, on July 16, 1969, Apollo 11 launched from Cape Kennedy. Millions of people watched the first manned mission to land on the moon. On July 20, Commander Neil Armstrong and Lunar Module Pilot Edwin "Buzz" Aldrin, Jr. became the first humans to walk on the lunar surface. President Richard Nixon said that, "For one priceless moment in the whole history of man, all of the people on this Earth are truly one."

In direct contradiction to the president's claim of humanity's oneness, Black people were protesting the $5.4 billion dollars spent on this competition with the Soviet Union to dominate outer space. Black newspapers and radio stations criticized the money spent on the Apollo mission while millions of Black people fought poverty and injustice on the ground.

Reverend Ralph David Abernathy, head of the Southern Christian Leadership Conference (SCLC), led a protest of two dozen Black families to the fence of Cape Kennedy in Florida. They were accompanied by mules, who symbolized rural poverty. Rev. Abernathy's sign stated, "$12 a day to feed an astronaut. We could feed a starving child for $8." At the rally, he said, "We may go on from this day to Mars and to Jupiter and even to the heavens beyond, but as long as racism, poverty and hunger and war prevail on the Earth, we as a civilized nation have failed."

On the radio, Sly and the Family Stone, Curtis Mayfield and the Impressions, and others described Black-White tensions in melodic, harmonious soundtracks for the times.

In the midst of this hostile back-and-forth, I tried to calculate where Jews and their coded slur of schvartze fit into the picture. While many Jews were hustling hard to win the assimilation game, in the late 1960s, they weren't yet fully accepted into the majority culture. Despite name changes, nose jobs and adopting anti-Black attitudes, Jews were sometimes still denied entrance into the gates of full-fledged Whiteness. Along with Black people, they were often excluded from White spaces such as elite country clubs. I was heartened by the sight and stories of Jewish people who worked alongside Black people in the Civil Rights Movement; that kind of solidarity helped soften the sting of racism and anti-Semitism with the image of a unified struggle.

Other than my racist Hebrew School classmate, most Jews didn't reject me. Once they'd vetted me with the "which parent?" qualifier to determine my ranking as a "real" Jew, I was allowed access. But unlike Black people, they never reached out to welcome or embrace me. They never indicated that I was part of their "us" or "we." I wasn't sure how they would receive or respond to the non-Jewish parts of my background. Because of that and the dynamics of the slur schvartze, while I appreciated the Jewish part of my background, I defined it mostly in relation to my mother and not in any sense of belonging to the larger collective.

The bigger mystery was my Native American ancestry. Mom said that both of Dad's parents—who died before I was born—had "a lot of" Native in their bloodlines. I never knew which tribes contributed to my mix, and nobody gave me any history, folklore or traditions to relate to. Dad never mentioned anything about it to me, so I wasn't sure what it meant to him. I saw hints of my paternal grandparents as the summer sun heightened the red undertones in my complexion. I felt it among the many textures of my hair. But without details or contact, there was no tangible way to connect to that part of me.

Seattle and the Pacific Northwest were rich in Native American history and culture. The first time I came face to face with an actual Native was downtown near the Pike Place Market. I studied the men and women with proud features and deep bronze complexions, longing to feel a bond. It didn't help that the few I saw seemed destitute, often drunk or high. Some were slouched on benches or passed out on the ground. I spoke, but they didn't respond, except to sometimes extend a hand for me to drop coins into. I felt sad and frustrated that they weren't trying to fight back the way that Black people did. I knew there had to be Indians somewhere who were strong, proud and standing up for themselves, but it would be years before I met them in person and learned more about their active resistance against the forces that had caused them so much pain.

As a teen, I wondered how my destiny was tied to my different familial strands, and whether it was natural to feel a stronger bond with some parts than with others. While considering how to reconcile the bloodlines of three continents, I realized that the common thread among my ancestors was their shared histories of being relentlessly persecuted simply because of who they were. I started to appreciate that they had survived great oppression. They fought, they escaped, they endured. Best of all, they had proven themselves to be indestructible. That was the gift they passed on to Greg and me. It was reassuring to know that, no matter what anyone thought about how I identified, or how disappointed they were in the way I moved through the world, my powerful ancestral inheritance would never let me down.

Chapter 15: Choice of Colors

I started high school with Curtis Mayfield's latest hit, "Choice of Colors," running nonstop through my mind. The lyrics inquiring about options and preferences resonated deeply with me as I faced the challenges of learning yet another new school where I had no roots or strong connections.

On the first day, I got to know two girls from the neighborhood. Michelle and Carolyn, who were at my bus stop. They'd been friends since elementary school and we all felt the awkwardness of my presence. At first, they held back, checking me out. I chatted and smiled to put them at ease, and soon we were hanging out.

Both were brown-skinned, slender, and taller than me. Michelle was high energy, witty and fast-talking, with a tough exterior and almond eyes behind stylish glasses. Carolyn was a beauty, with a heart-shaped face, big, innocent eyes, and cupid-bow lips. She was quiet and soft-spoken with a goofy sense of humor. I was as awkward as ever—light, bright and damn-near-White with my frizzy "That Girl" flip and long bangs. Now that we could finally wear pants to school, my uniform was bell-bottom jeans and a huge green army jacket that I wore inside and outside, no matter the weather or temperature.

The bus ride to Roosevelt was shorter than the one to Jane Addams, and the school wasn't as frigid or foreboding. We had the advantage of coming behind Black students in the higher grades who'd paved the way, so most of the White students didn't seem as put-off by our presence. There were some familiar faces from Meany, which provided some comfort. The teachers seemed more preoccupied with managing hundreds of hormonally crazed teenagers than with our color.

High school brought another new experience: my first real bully—a girl on the bus who seemed to single me out for dirty looks and hostile vibes. She was on the lighter side of stick-around-brown with beady eyes, a prominent nose, an unimpressive Afro and lips that seemed stuck in a sneer.

I didn't even notice Bully until Carolyn and Michelle pointed her out, whispering that she "wanted to get me." That didn't make sense: I wasn't cute, cool, or popular and if Bully had a boyfriend, he wasn't trying to talk to me. I wondered why she'd go to the trouble of hating somebody she'd never met.

When shooting me dirty looks and muttering things like "she thinks she's so cute" half under her breath didn't get a response, Bully took it up a notch. "Yella bitch," she hissed one day as I passed her on the bus.

I paused, knowing those were fighting words. Trouble was, I didn't care as much about her as she seemed to care about me. So, I did what Mom advised me to do when Greg tried to get on my nerves: I ignored her.

But she was determined. Days later, Bully pushed in front of me in line to get on the bus after school. She whirled to face me, fire shooting from her eyes. "Half-breed," she spat.

I laughed in her face. "Half-breed? Is that all you've got?" When she looked shocked, I added, "No points for stating the obvious. Better luck next time." I threw in a smirk and flounced to my seat as the bus supervisor told her to sit down.

I figured she thought that being Mixed made me an easy target, and felt annoyed that she viewed me as a stereotype. I was also disappointed that her so-called hatred of me felt too trite and generic to warrant an equivalent response from me. I compared Bully to Tim at Addams, reflecting how a White male felt compelled to attack my Blackness, while a Black female felt obligated to challenge it. I figured if I'd had a White bully, it was only fair that I had a Black one to even things out. I waited to see whether she could compete with Tim's use of the ultimate weapon.

Riding the school bus was cool until Michelle, Carolyn and I learned that it wasn't our only option. There were no rules against walking to the city bus stop near school and riding downtown to shop, eat, and hang out before we went home. When we had a little money, we checked out the fashion stores, thrilled to learn that we could put things we liked on layaway at places like Lerner's and Jay Jacobs. We strolled the aisles of Woolworth's to look at cheap costume jewelry and devour super greasy fried chicken.

Me in high school with my "That Girl" flip and no afro

One day on the city bus home, we sat near a Black man and White woman. They held hands, her head resting on his shoulder. I hadn't noticed them until Michelle nudged me hard and asked, "What do you think of that?"

"Nothing," I answered.

Michelle rolled her eyes. Carolyn shook her head. I guessed they disapproved of the couple and wanted to see where I stood on the matter, but since there wasn't a Mixed child sitting with them, I wasn't interested enough to bother forming an opinion.

High school also brought my first heart-thumping crush. Simon was an upperclassman, tall and light-skinned with a towering reddish-brown Afro, piercing dark eyes, a shy, crooked smile, and a gentle bop to his long-legged stride. He was a junior, and he didn't ride the bus because his best friend had a car.

I wanted to attract his attention, but had no idea how to start. Then I learned that he was dating a White girl. Every time I saw them, I was haunted by the voices of all the boys and men claiming that White girls were superior.

The next time Michelle asked me what I thought about an anonymous Mixed couple we saw downtown, Simon and his girlfriend flashed through my mind. His choice felt personal. I followed Michelle's hard stare to the ebony and ivory duo that had her attention. "He could do better," I said. She nodded her approval, thinking I was talking about the strangers in front of us.

Michelle's question made me wonder what kind of things people had thought or said about my parents when they were together. It was strange knowing that I'd been created by that kind of two-toned love while I tried to form opinions about what made people want to cross those lines.

Chapter 16: Black and White and What?

My crush on Simon still raged, though he was still with his girlfriend. When I learned he was Mixed, I wondered if that automatically made us compatible. Not knowing how to flirt or make him notice me, I wrote sappy love poems and sent him telepathic messages, hoping for a miracle.

I thought I knew where I fell on the scale of attractiveness, but an incident at Carolyn's house caught me off guard. We were hanging out there after school when some of her many family members stopped by. The weather was warmer than usual, so I'd ditched my ever-present bell-bottom jeans for a miniskirt and draped my green army jacket over my arm. We stood with our backs to the front door, watching one of Carolyn's little brothers acting up in the kitchen. As we laughed at his antics, an unfamiliar woman's voice broke through: "Would you look at that? She's just so pretty!" A chorus of male and female voices rose in excited agreement.

Carolyn, who was usually the target of such compliments, was in front of me, so I looked around to see which one of her sisters they were talking about. I was shocked to see all eyes on me. I wasn't used to being called "pretty." I was the goofy one; everybody knew that. On a good day, somebody might call me "kind of cute" and leave it at that.

My head pounded and my gut clenched as they stared, transfixed. I wanted to escape. Just like that time when Dad bragged that Greg and I were "pretty," I knew the loaded compliment was strictly because of my pale skin and long hair. I couldn't accept it as confirmation of genuine attractiveness. This focus on my appearance, which I couldn't fully understand or articulate, had my emotions in turmoil.

I felt guilty for enjoying the stab of pleasure at somebody thinking I looked good. If only Simon could hear them, I thought, maybe he'd finally notice me. Maybe he'd even agree with them.

Walking home, I thought about how Bully seemed to hate me and thought that maybe I was a stand-in for the "pretty" girl in her family or neighborhood—the one who got all the attention and compliments just because she fit the stereotype of what everybody was trained to admire. I wondered how many times Bully had felt overlooked or left out. I realized that if I could attract undeserved praise for my looks, I could attract hostility for them too.

I was learning that people could be criticized for all kinds of things. With school busing came the idea that being brainy and having White friends made you a traitor to Black people. I wasn't sure what to think when that standard was applied to a Mixed person.

LeAnn, a super smart brown-skinned Mixed girl, and her younger sister lived down the hill from me. Their father was a musician, and they were part of the Jazz Baby community that shaped my early life. At school, LeAnn was known for earning top grades. She hung out with mostly White and Asian kids. I realized I'd never seen her talking with a Black person outside of her family, even on the bus.

One day, some of the kids on the bus demanded to know why she was "acting White." They accused her of thinking she was better than everyone else. Some called her an Uncle Tom and a traitor. "Stop it!" I yelled. "She's Mixed, that's all. It's not the same!" Bully shot me a look full of daggers, but so far, she'd been all talk and no action. Nobody was hitting LeAnn physically, but the words landed hard. As panic raced across LeAnn's face, I tried to catch her eye, to reassure her that she wasn't alone. But she never looked my way.

LeAnn's family lived at the bottom of our steep hill, behind a fence with a "Dead End" sign that had arrows pointing left and right, directing cars to turn north or south. When we were little, we played softball and kickball in front of that fence, with the sign serving as home plate. Sometimes we'd knock on the door and ask if LeAnn and her sister could come out to play. They usually turned us down. When I visited their house with Mom, I was impressed by how serious LeAnn was as she practiced complex classical European music on the piano. She seemed mature beyond her years, uninterested in the childish games we played outside her house. She rarely spoke to us, and when she did, it was in sharp, clipped tones. She was different from the rest of us Mixed kids on the block, but I figured LeAnn had a right to her preferences.

What kind of choices did people like LeAnn and me really have though?

What were the options if both of us were being bullied for who we were? Or the boys already liked White girls better than all of us? And if our blended identities came with rules that other people made up for their convenience?

I struggled to see the options that Mom, Dad and others imagined for me. I wondered why everyone couldn't simply be themselves without being questioned, bullied or dissected by others. I wanted any White person who spat nigger or any Jewish person who said schvartze to feel the marrow-deep ache of those slurs. I wanted to stop hearing so many Black boys and men insist that White girls and women were "better."

I wanted something more than either/or. I couldn't name what that something was, but the yearning consumed me.

Sometimes Michelle and Carolyn walked right past me in the school hallway like I was invisible. I'd yell their names, and they'd turn around, smiling sheepishly, and say, "Oops, we thought you were a White girl." But when I wore red, they'd see me and say, "Wow, that color makes you look Blacker." I rolled my eyes and thought that all of this could be solved with an Afro.

It still didn't occur to me that my appearance could pose a danger to my safety. One afternoon, our Roosevelt basketball team was playing Garfield—the cool, mostly Black school that we would be attending if we hadn't been racially transferred. We went to cheer for our friend and star Roosevelt player, Johnny Vallot, the Creole kid with the winning moves and bouncing Afro. He was tight with my crush Simon, so I hoped to see him, too.

Roosevelt was beating Garfield so badly that their players started attacking the referees and our cheerleaders. Tensions were high, with rumors of fights erupting around us. Michelle, Carolyn and I ran outside and stood in the winter air, debating whether we should stay or leave. I scanned the crowd for Simon.

Then a female voice shouted, "Let's get Whitey!"

I looked to see who she was talking about, and saw her staring at me. I smirked, confident she'd come to her senses and recognize that I was "sumthin." Her friends joined her and they moved towards us. I shouted, "I'm not—" when Michelle pushed me towards the street.

"Run, Terri!" she screamed. "Just go!"

I wasn't athletic, I wasn't in shape, I wasn't dressed for it. But I sprinted north on 23rd Avenue like rabid dogs were chasing me. I ran the whole mile and a half through red lights, dodging cars and ignoring frantically blaring horns. The sweat stung my eyes as I panted, gulping the chilled night air like it was water. I stumbled a few times, but I didn't slow down until I collapsed in a disheveled, exhausted heap on the front steps of our house, my eyes peeled for anyone who might have followed me.

It took a good five minutes for my heart to regain its normal rhythm and five more for me to summon the strength to climb the steps, find my key and unlock the door. "We won the game," I gasped as Mom looked me over, eyes full of questions. I wished I could tell her what had happened, but I knew she viewed Garfield as dangerous territory and wouldn't be happy that I'd been hanging out there. Even if I told her, would she have understood the complexities I had to navigate? How could she, when I was struggling to make sense of them myself? Mom was always stressed, bringing home extra work to make ends meet, losing sleep over which bills to pay, and worrying about my disappointing academic performance. I didn't want her to feel bad about having Mixed kids.

Instead, I flashed what I hoped was a reassuring smile and made a beeline to the bathroom where I peeled off my clothes and took a long hot shower. I used the edge of a towel to wipe the steam from the bathroom mirror and stared at myself: the startling contrast of dark hair, pale skin, deep brown eyes and flushed cheeks. My brain was still catching up to my body, thankful for my narrow escape.

I wasn't mad. I wasn't sad. I was grateful to Michelle for saving my ass. I calculated my racial math. How Black was my soul? My state of mind? Which was more important—what I looked like, what I knew myself to be, or what others presumed based on a casual glance? I could have been beaten and bloodied because this time, in the heat of rage, nobody thought to ask or wonder. They just assumed and were ready to jump me.

The racial tensions wracking our country that were reflected in our schools went both ways. I'd heard about how Garfield students were being called racist names, threatened, and even attacked when their teams played at the White schools.

Later, our school basketball star Johnny Vallot told us that he'd dodged bricks and rocks after that game at Garfield. Rather than walk a few blocks to his Central-Area home, he'd raced to ride the team bus all the way back across town to Roosevelt. "I grew up with those guys; they're from my neighborhood," he said sadly about the Garfield students. "But they were throwing bricks at my head."

They knew Johnny, that he was as Black as them, and still tried to attack him. It was one thing to be threatened by strangers who didn't know where you fell on the racial scale. It was worse to be attacked by your own people because they identified you with the enemy and branded you a traitor.

On the bus, LeAnn was stoic about being called a traitor, an Uncle Tom and a wannabe White girl. I still tried to defend her, but nobody listened to me. I figured that if I felt Blacker than I looked, it made sense for LeAnn to feel Whiter than she looked. It seemed that's how the dice rolled when you were Mixed.

LeAnn and I got off the bus at the same stop and walked across the street together. I wanted to tell her that I was sorry, assure her I didn't think she was a Tom, and that she deserved to have a choice. But she never looked at or spoke to me. She never acknowledged how I tried to stick up for her. She just walked, back straight, chin raised, down the hill to her house behind the fence with the "Dead End" sign and the arrows pointing both ways.

The 1950 Census

The 1950 census racial categories were W for White, Neg for Negro, Ind for American Indian, Jap for Japanese, Chi for Chinese, Fil for Filipino, and Other race (with details spelled out). The Hindu and Korean categories were dropped, and "American" was added to "Indian."

This was the first census to try to separately count some tri-racial mixtures of White, Negro, and American Indian living in small communities in the eastern U.S. These communities had existed for some time and were locally recognized by special names, such as Siouian or Croatan, Moor, and Tunica. They were counted as "Nonwhite" in the "Other race" category.

The 1960 Census

The 1960 census was the first to utilize questionnaires delivered by mail carriers to each residential address. To accommodate self-identification, the wording of the race question changed to "Is this person--White, Negro, American Indian, Japanese, Chinese, Filipino, Hawaiian, Part Hawaiian, Aleut, Eskimo, etc.?"

This is the first time that Hawaiian, Part-Hawaiian, Aleut, and Eskimo were counted separately. The Eskimo and Aleut categories applied just to Alaska, and the Hawaiian and Part-Hawaiian just to Hawaii, both of which became states in 1959.

For those who did not mail in the questionnaires, the 1960 census enumerators were instructed to record:

> *Puerto Ricans, Mexicans, or other persons of Latin American descent as "White" unless they were definitely of Negro, Indian, or another non-white race. Enumerators also classified such responses as Italian, Portuguese, Polish, Syrian, Lebanese, and other European and Near-Eastern nationalities as White. Negroes and persons of mixed White and Negro parentage were marked as Negro. A person of mixed Indian and Negro blood was classified as Negro unless the enumerator knew that the Indian blood very definitely predominated and that the person was regarded in the community as an Indian. The enumerator marked "American Indian" for full-blooded Indians, and also for persons of mixed White and Indian blood if he could determine that they were enrolled on an Indian tribal or agency roll, or if he knew that they were regarded as Indians in the community where they lived.*

Chapter 17: Twice as Good

It was increasingly difficult to focus on schoolwork while trying to untangle how race and rage collided in the world. No teachers or lessons ever acknowledged everything that was going on around us—or inside of us either.

Not all of the students were in the Voluntary Racial Transfer program as a form of punishment, like I was. Some said their parents had signed them up because they'd get a better education in the faraway White schools than the ones in our neighborhoods. I didn't see any difference between the quality of teachers, classrooms or lessons at Seward, Meany, Addams or Roosevelt. That rationale struck me as another example of believing that everything White was automatically better. Or as I'd heard older Black folks say, "The White man's ice is colder." I knew that White people usually demanded and felt entitled to the best of everything, and reasoned that White parents wouldn't send their children from the north end schools to inner-city Meany Middle School and Garfield High School if those schools were really inferior. This made me even more suspicious of the Voluntary Racial Transfer program.

The biggest lesson I learned from integrating these schools was how to decode the propaganda of White superiority. In that environment, it was easy to see that, like us, White kids ranged from super smart to ordinary to kind of doofus. They had teen angst, acne and attitudes, just like us. What set them apart was their belief that they were inherently better than us. This was underscored by everything we were taught in school. It was the law of the land, never questioned or challenged in any way.

From time to time, different kids on the bus would share how their parents had drilled into them that they had to work twice as hard and be twice as good as White people to make it in the world. I wondered why Mom had never said that to us.

When I asked her about it, her face softened with memory.

"That's what my father—your Zadie—used to say to me: that I had to work twice as hard and be twice as good as the gentiles. He learned that in Russia, where they were persecuted for being Jews, and he believed it about this country, too. Your Zadie was a wonderful salesman. He worked around the clock. Sometimes we had money and sometimes we didn't. But I saw what working 'twice as hard' looked like—the exhaustion in his eyes, the creases in his proud face, how he limped on sore feet. And still he insisted that all of us—my sisters, my brothers, and me—would have to do the same. To prove that we were good enough, that we belonged in this great land. But I couldn't believe that the gentiles were better than us. And I didn't think it was fair to expect me to do more just to be seen as less, no matter how hard I worked. So that's why I've never said it to you or Greg. You are not less. No matter what people think or say. And you don't have to prove anything to them either."

Mom also said that "People claim they're superior because they really feel inferior." She never specified any one group when she said it, but I wondered if that was why White people worked overtime to convince themselves and everyone else that their natural position was on top of everyone else.

I was reminded of that belief by a classmate in typing class. I was a pretty fast typist, but Jan, a petite blonde girl who sat next to me, was faster. We banged away on those clunky black manual typewriters, racing each other to type more words per minute. I was usually faster, but she had fewer errors. I thought she was cool until the day she turned to me and asked, ""Terri, what um, nationality, are you?" she asked, blushing as her eyes bored into mine.

"My nationality is American. You know, as in U.S. citizen."

"I mean um, what are you?"

"Black and—"

"But you don't have to be, right?"

"What are you talking about?"

"Wouldn't you rather be, you know, just regular?"

"Regular? You mean White?"

"Yeah. I mean, no offense, but wouldn't that be better than being

Black?"

I shook my head. "White isn't better than Black. I just want to be what I am. And for people to stop asking me stupid-ass questions."

"Look, I didn't mean—"

I hurried off, suddenly weary. After that day, I still sat next to her, but I no longer spoke or raced to beat her typing speed.

Weeks later, I got another lesson in whiteness. After gym class, I was dressing near a group of White girls in the locker room. My back was to them, and they were too caught up in their conversation to notice me. I didn't pay attention to their conversation until one of them announced loudly, "I'm so tired of them. They're everywhere now. They even think they can be cheerleaders." I froze, thinking of the girls on the bus who'd just tried out for the cheerleading squad.

"Yeah. They come here from their ghettos and ruin everything," another said.

I thought about confronting these girls, but I was outnumbered. And I wanted to hear how far they'd go.

"Some of them seem like good students," another girl offered.

"But not as good as us," the first girl quickly countered.

"I sure wish I could dance like them though," a third girl laughed. I bit back the bile that rose in my throat, determined to hear every word.

"I have a friend who's bused to Garfield, poor thing," a fourth girl said. "She said she's scared to even go inside the girl's lav to pee, so she has to hold it 'til she gets home!"

Their voices rose in dismay as they grabbed their belongings and walked out.

I sat in place until the locker room was empty, replaying everything I'd overheard until it was committed to memory. Then I rushed to tell Michelle and Carolyn what I'd heard. Instead of being impressed with my reporting, they interrupted before I could finish.

"Did you get in their faces?" Michelle asked.

"I thought about it, but I wanted to hear what—"

"You should have said something," Carolyn scolded.

"But then they wouldn't have said it!" I was frustrated that Michelle and Carolyn didn't appreciate the insights I was sharing.

It took a rude awakening to help me understand a much more important difference in the ways that my friends and I moved through the world.

On one of our downtown detours, I wanted to eat something other than the fried chicken we usually grabbed at Woolworths. The Bon Marché department store was a step up from J.C. Penney's, but not as fancy as Nordstrom or Frederick & Nelson. When the Bon had a good sale, Mom would take us shopping, followed by lunch in their café. I liked the chicken croissant sandwiches and loved feeling a little fancy and grown-up when Mom and I ate there.

I told Michelle and Carolyn about the Bon café. They looked at each other uneasily.

"I've never been there," Carolyn said.

"You'll like it, I swear."

"I don't think we have enough money," Michelle said, fidgeting.

"I have a twenty."

They finally gave in but were unusually subdued as we moved through the store aisles onto the elevator. I noticed how uncomfortable they looked and smiled thinking how much they were going to enjoy sitting and having a nice meal instead of gobbling down delicious but greasy chicken parts.

A waitress led us to a booth and sat us down. She took our order, looking at and speaking only to me. I thought it was because she recognized me from my visits with Mom.

She ignored us while serving many other people who came in after we did. We sat, stomachs growling, waiting impatiently for our food for half an hour before Michelle stood up. "Let's go, Terri," she said softly, as if she didn't want to hurt my feelings. "They don't want us here."

I knew she was right, but I didn't want her to be. "Let's give them a couple more minutes," I pleaded, my eyes seeking the waitress. She passed by us to serve others, never glancing our way.

"I'd rather have Woolworth's anyway," Carolyn muttered as the waitress marched past us again. I hung my head, biting back tears of anger and shame.

As we walked out, the waitress called, "Hey! What about your sandwiches?" I shook my head and flipped her the bird.

Even the comforting crunch of Woolworth's greasy fried chicken didn't lighten our mood.

"It's all right," Carolyn assured me. "You didn't know."

Yeah, but that was the problem, I thought. I should have known. I should have realized that my skin allowed me to move through the world unaware of certain things. I'd subjected my friends to unnecessary humiliation because I never thought that going to that restaurant with them would be different than going with my mom—where I got to pass for "just people."

I could assume a friendly café waitress and a delicious sandwich placed gently in front of me with a warm smile and a question about whether there was anything else I desired. Michelle and Carolyn could not assume the same. I wasn't sure whether Celia or LeAnn could either.

There was much more to racism than Jim Crow, Klan members in sheets, crosses burning and Black bodies swinging from trees. There were layers far more complicated than I'd considered. Even without any obvious "White only" signs, the department store café had spoken loud and clear.

The next few times Michelle and Carolyn walked past me in the school hallways, then doubled back at the sound of my voice, I swallowed my customary annoyance. I didn't yet know how to fully make sense of it, but I was starting to realize that the flip side of my inconvenient appearance was the privilege I had never been so painfully aware of, or felt in such a gut-wrenching way. My eyes were forced open. I'd been unconscious about how much that racial doubt translated to a kind of access that excluded others who didn't look like me—or how I would be excluded if the truth of my identity was more obvious to certain people.

Not all White people thought I was one of them, though. People often stared at Mom, Greg and me. When I'd fidget and scowl, Mom assured me that they were looking because I was "so pretty, so exotic." I knew that "exotic" meant funny-looking. When strangers studied us too closely, I waited until Mom looked the other way, then cut my eyes at them and stuck out my tongue to let them know I was hip to their game.

The next time the Bon Marché had a sale, I dreaded following Mom into the café for our lunch. The same waitress who'd been so ugly when I'd come in with my friends was all sunshine and smiles for Mom and me. I realized that she didn't know I was the same person who'd come in with two Black girls. I mumbled my order, refusing to meet her eyes. When my beloved sandwich came, I took a few bites and pushed it away.

I looked around at the other faces in the café—mostly White, a couple of Asian—and wondered: How could I tell my mother that everything on the menu came with a secret side order of hate?

Chapter 18: And I'm Super-Bad!

The coolest thing you could be in the early 1970s was "bad," which meant good. Sometimes we had to specify our use of the adjective. The claim that something was bad might spark the query, "You mean good-bad or bad-bad?" "Super-bad" meant super-good, which was better than "groovy" or "out-of-sight." It was the epitome of everything an awkward teen could hope to be.

Bully didn't say much to me at school, and we never had any classes together. She saved her attacks for the bus. One day she pushed her chest out and said, "You think you're bad, huh?

"That depends," I said. "You mean good-bad or bad-bad?"

A few kids seated nearby started to laugh. "Whoosh, she got you!"

Her eyes narrowed. "You're so confused, you don't even know what you are!"

I rolled my eyes, still disappointed by the triteness of her intended insults. "I know exactly what I am. You're the one who's confused."

She didn't say anything, just sneered and stomped off. If she wanted me to fight, she just had to call me "Peola" from "Imitation of Life," like poor Ken at the YMCA had, and I'd tear her up. But she hadn't figured that out.

Then I learned a shocking secret about Bully's family. "See that girl?" Carolyn said one day, pointing at a petite brunette with the kind of tan our White classmates got when they went skiing. She seemed vaguely familiar but I couldn't place her. Carolyn said the girl was Bully's first cousin. "She's Mixed like you."

"No way," I said, squinting hard at her, the way people did at me. Her skin was a few shades darker than mine, her hair longer, straighter and lighter brown. I wondered if people pelted her with questions and rules like they did me. And if Bully really was her cousin, how they got along.

Now that I knew, I was fascinated by the passing girl. I watched her closely. Her eyes never seemed to land on the Black kids; she didn't exhibit any sense of kinship or connection that I could see. She wasn't part of the racial transfer program. If she really was passing, why didn't the Black kids seem to care?

"Wait a minute," I wanted to demand. "Doesn't that make her a traitor? Or a Tom? Or worse?" I couldn't reconcile Bully messing with me or LeAnn while her own cousin was imitating life right under everyone's noses.

Maybe she wasn't passing for White—which seemed to require deception and betrayal of one's own truth. Maybe she just lived around White people and blended in so easily that nobody questioned what she was, pushed her to explain herself, or pressed her to make choices.

I wondered where the lines of truth and deception crossed and what it was like to be White—how diligently I'd have to work to convince myself of my superiority. How often I'd sharpen my sense of self at the expense of those who were "different."

I thought about how Malcolm X's pilgrimage to Mecca with Muslims of different colors changed his view of White people as devils, and race as the great divide:

> "On this pilgrimage, what I have seen and experienced has forced me to rearrange much of my thought-patterns previously held, and to toss aside some of my previous conclusions … During the past eleven days here in the Muslim world, I have eaten from the same plate, drunk from the same glass, and slept in the same bed (or on the same rug) – while praying to the same God – with fellow Muslims, whose eyes were the bluest of blue, whose hair was the blondest of blonde, and whose skin was the whitest of white … We were truly all the same (brothers) --because their belief in one God had removed the 'white' from their minds, the 'white' from their behavior, and the 'white' from their attitude."

Excerpted from The Autobiography of Malcolm X, as told to Alex Haley, Ballantine Books, 1964

Based on what he wrote, I thought that if Blackness was truly a state of mind, maybe Whiteness was too. But could any Mixed person enter or exit either of those states at will?

At the end of the year, my blonde classmate from typing class shocked me by writing in my yearbook:

"Terri, if those questions I asked you about Black and White offended you, I'm sorry. I was just asking. It might have seemed like it was really important as to how I would treat you—but it wasn't. This is kind of a sad thing to put in an annual, but it has been bugging me. Love, J."

The world was sending so many contradictory and confusing messages, with no easy way to decode them. Though I read voraciously and searched eagerly, I'd never found a single book about someone like me. I'd never seen a character I could relate to on TV or in the movies. I longed for my early years when being in a tight-knit community of Mixed couples and children allowed me to feel normal, regular, accepted without conditions or challenges. To fit in rather than stand out.

I wondered if the Black kids didn't care about Bully's cousin passing because her insides and her outsides matched. Mine didn't match and neither did LeAnn's—we were opposites. Would life have been simpler if our cultural affiliations were more in line with the way we looked?

While we studied DNA in science class and the way that our families' traits were passed down to us, I thought about how that worked with Mixed people. If we inherited physical features, personality traits, quirks, habits, and other things from the folks in our bloodline, did it make sense that we might also naturally lean one way or the other when it came to racial or cultural identity? Maybe our preferences, our natural tendencies, weren't choices but acts of nature. Maybe we weren't supposed to make sense to anybody but ourselves.

Chapter 19: Bold Soul Sister

In August 1970, Angela Davis's image was everywhere, her glorious Afro and stunning face a symbol of the revolution brewing throughout Black America. She'd become world famous when "Soledad Brother" and Black Panther George Jackson's seventeen-year-old brother, Jonathan Jackson, went into the Marin County, California, courtroom with weapons. In a desperate attempt to free his big brother George from prison, Jonathan disarmed the county sheriff, then provided guns to three Black inmates from San Quentin—the defendant, Willie McClain, and witnesses Ruchell Magee and William Christmas—with hopes of freeing them. After the quartet of armed men took the prosecutor and judge as hostages, Jonathan demanded that George and two other Soledad Brothers be released from prison, with a plane to fly them to Cuba. The foursome moved through the courthouse taking sheriff's guns, then to the parking lot where Jonathan fired several shots into the air.

But their plan was doomed. Both the California Highway Patrol and San Quentin prison had been tipped off and were waiting. As Jonathan and his comrades piled into a van, the cops and guards opened fire, shooting and killing Jonathan, the judge and two of the inmates. Ruchell Magee lived and the prosecutor survived, paralyzed for life from his wounds.

Watching this tragedy, called "Black August," on the news, I wondered if this was what the Revolution was supposed to look like. Angela Davis had already lost her teaching job at the University of California Los Angeles for admitting her membership in the Communist Party. Now, she was accused of providing the four guns that Jonathan Jackson had taken into the courtroom. She was also accused of having ridden in the van days before the shootout.

When authorities couldn't find her, she was charged with murder, kidnapping and intent to evade prosecution. Angela Davis became the second "Black militant" on the FBI's Most Wanted List, along with H. Rap Brown. "Free Angela!" posters and chants spread across the country. Superstar Aretha Franklin publicly announced her support.

By late summer, Angela Davis was running from the FBI, which had declared the Black Panther Party America's most "dangerous extremist organization." Elmer and Aaron Dixon had taught us about the FBI's counterintelligence COINTEL program designed to take down the Panthers and other Black leaders. It was the same program that had targeted Malcolm X and Dr. King. The Civil Rights Act might have challenged Jim Crow, Black people could vote and interracial marriage was no longer illegal, but fighting for justice was still viewed as a threat. Sometimes it seemed like America didn't want Black people to live or be free.

While it wasn't clear how the Revolution for Black power and equality would unfold, having an Afro was pretty much required. And I was out of luck. My brother Greg often got me to braid, blow out and comb his into a perfect cloud, while my traitorous tresses continued to mock my "Power to the People" spirit.

The solution arrived unexpectedly. On Labor Day weekend before the start of the new school year, Mom's Jewish friend Saralee visited from Los Angeles with three of her four gorgeous daughters, whose late father was Black. They were the first people I'd met who were the same mix as Greg and me. I wished I looked like them with caramel skin, golden-tinged hair and long-lashed green eyes.

Saralee was a hairdresser who promised she could give me an Afro without a smelly, harsh chemical perm. The night before the first day of my junior year, she rinsed my hair in apple cider vinegar, and then painstakingly twisted a few strands at a time around dozens of tiny perm rods. It took her hours and I'm sure her hands ached. My scalp was on fire, so I slept upright in a chair, happy to sacrifice for the cause.

I was up extra-early the next morning, and Saralee patiently unrolled the dozens of perm rods, leaving my head covered in tight coils. She picked them into an Afro almost as majestic as Greg's. I looked so much like him that I applied some of Mom's lipstick, mascara and eyeliner so nobody would mistake me for a boy. I slipped into my new first-day-of-school miniskirt, turtleneck and platform shoes. I channeled my inner Angela Davis and strode to the bus stop with my head held high. I felt grown. I felt powerful. For once, I felt like my appearance was closer to matching my insides.

Carolyn and Michelle gasped in amazement, reaching out to touch my new hair and ask how I'd achieved the impossible. Smiling mysteriously, I climbed the stairs to the bus, strolling slowly to the back, taking an extra moment to look Bully straight in the eye and flick her a petty half-smile. Showered in compliments, I felt bold, beautiful, invincible. Nobody could tell me nothin'.

My euphoria lasted until we walked from the bus to the school building. I felt the first drop of rain hit my forehead. Then my neck. By the time I made it to my first class, my hair was falling into its natural state, my newfound confidence drooping with it. I found a rubber band and pulled the unruly mess into a lump that bounced against the back of my neck to remind me of my short-lived glory.

I waited for Bully to ridicule my humiliating hair disaster, but she didn't seem to notice. Maybe she'd lost interest in bullying, or sensed that I could flash on her about her passing cousin, Carla. She still gave me dirty looks and spat the word "yella" every now and then, but even that felt half-hearted.

As the leaves reddened and crisped into fall, Carolyn and Michelle shared exciting news: Some students were forming a Black Student Union (BSU). My heart raced—I looked forward to something like the Black Panther Party's Political Education sessions where we discussed Angela Davis, who had just been found and arrested by the FBI, Mao Tse Tung, or The Autobiography of Malcolm X. I briefly wished I could recreate my 'fro, but Saralee had taken her hair-styling magic and her gorgeous daughters back to Los Angeles.

The day of the first BSU meeting, classes seemed to drag on forever. I'd even worn red, remembering Michelle and Carolyn saying that it made me look Blacker. Once the last bell rang, I ran to my locker, shoved in my school books, grabbed my copies of The Panther Paper, and hurried to the BSU meeting room. I slid into my seat with an expectant smile, surprised to see Bully standing in front of the room holding a clipboard. "I call the first meeting of the Roosevelt High School Black Student Union to order."

Then she looked at me. "You. Get out of here!"

I laughed. "I don't think so."

"This is the BLACK Student Union. It's for us. Not you."

I scanned the room, my confused gaze landing on Michelle and Carolyn. They looked unhappy, but didn't say a word. Nobody else moved or spoke.

Dear Reader,

Thank you SO MUCH for your support of SWIRL GIRL! It means *everything* to me. I hope you enjoy the book, and look forward to your review on AlchemyMediaPublishing.com.

Since we were suddenly thrust into Corona Quarantine, we couldn't do the planned final proofreading of the manuscript. As a result, there are some typos which we're working to correct in the next printing.

Please accept my apology. I hope the missed edits don't interfere with your reading experience.

With Love and Gratitude,

TaRessa Stovall 2020

My face flaming, I stood, grabbed my Black Panther papers, and stomped out, slamming the door behind me. The school bus had gone, so I walked, dazed and dizzy, to catch the city bus into downtown Seattle. I walked aimlessly along the grey streets, wondering how I could be Black enough to endure the bus rides, and be called a nigger, but not qualified to attend a BSU meeting. Bully had won this battle. I didn't know how I could show my face at school. She hadn't had to whup my butt. She'd drop-kicked my identity and gut-punched my pride. She'd pulled the Blacker-than-you card and claimed victory. And I had no way to fight back.

I was shocked because nobody had ever drawn such a definitive line before, with them on one side and me on the other. Endless questions raced in a circle until I realized that maybe I didn't belong in a Black Student Union. Maybe my love and knowledge of Malcolm X, Angela Davis and the Black Panthers weren't enough.

Maybe that line had been there, and I just hadn't noticed it. I wasn't growing up in a household run by a Black person. My appearance spared me from experiencing many of the racist indignities and attacks that were a routine part of being Black in America. I was stunned to realize that no matter what I felt inside, no matter where I was most at home, no matter where I pledged my racial allegiance, any random person held the power to grant or deny me entry into my chosen social group. I smiled bitterly, thinking Mom might be relieved that I wouldn't be joining the BSU. And Dad would ridicule me for wanting to join in the first place.

Wandering downtown, I saw a Black man with a hugely pregnant White woman. Next to them was a Mixed girl, about four years old. The girl stared so hard at me I wondered if she recognized our common bond. I thought about the baby in the woman's womb, worrying that neither of those children would have anyone to tell them what to expect from growing up Mixed. Even their parents wouldn't be able to help them.

For weeks, I couldn't get that little Mixed girl and her unborn sibling out of my mind. I'd always seen Mixed kids around, but now I noticed them and was consumed with wondering about their journeys. I longed to let them know that somebody understood what they would be going through, and lay awake at night planning what I could do to help prepare them for the world.

Inspired by my fledgling sense of purpose, I stowed my Black Panther papers and Malcolm X's autobiography in the back of my closet. At the public library, I searched frantically for any mention of Mixed people. There were references to the dozens of categories used to identify the many-colored people of

Brazil. I read about Mestizos in South America and Coloureds in South Africa, though it would be years before I l fully understood apartheid.

I spent hours in the library, poring over books in search of anything about people like me. I found "Mulatto"— a thorny word from the rapes of slavery defined as the unnatural mating of a horse and a mule symbolized by the offspring of interracial sex. It was a slur conceived to describe the DNA of trauma and unlikely survival. There was nothing in those seven letters to love or be proud of, nothing to warm my heart or sing to my soul.

Still, I savored the way it teased my eyes and curved off my tongue. Moo-lah-toe. I felt its bittersweet, complicated truths. I related to the jagged edges of its heartbreaking origins as a way for slave owners to track their human property, which connected that ugly past to my complicated present. Its three syllables embodied whip and chain, cotton and coin, broken flesh and battered souls. It leapfrogged over either/or to acknowledge my growing sense of "and." It was a declaration of wholeness—blood-soaked, reviled and tear-stained—that would not be denied. And it was still the lens through which much of the world viewed people like me.

I learned more about the popular "tragic" Mulatto. Outside of slave-turned-abolitionist Frederick Douglass, the only representation of Mixed people—especially women—were in the "Imitation of Life" mode with lives made tragic by their toxic rejection of self. I couldn't identify with that stereotype. The more I searched, the more frustrated I became at the lack of stories about Mixed people whose lives hadn't been ruined because they were "too Black to be White."

My new mission eclipsed Roosevelt High School's new Black Student Union. Bully still mumbled nonsense at me on the bus, but it barely registered. She could kick me out for not being Black enough, but neither she nor anyone else could squelch my new sense of possibility.

Then the universe sent another encouraging sign.

Ed Samuelsson came into our lives through the Big Brother program. Since Dad wasn't performing his fatherly duties, Mom signed Greg up to get a male mentor. Ed was a lanky, hip White guy with probing eyes, a knowing smile and a way of getting you to open up before you realized what was happening. Though he had a wife and children of his own and was busy running the Seattle Mental Health Institute, Ed always made time to come across town and hang out with Greg. His laid-back wisdom soon endeared him to all of us.

After I shared some of my convictions about being Mixed, Ed asked if

I'd help him out by leading a workshop about identity for some local mental health professionals. He said they were seeing more Mixed-race couples and children, and he thought it might help the therapists to hear from someone who had "a pretty strong sense of identity." I was shocked that an adult—especially an expert in human psychology—wasn't questioning, criticizing or challenging my way of seeing things.

Next thing I knew, I was giving advice to a room full of adults—mental health professionals—who were taking me seriously. They even took notes as I explained the need to recognize the whole child, without chopping him or her up into fractions or pressuring them to form an allegiance with one side or the other. I explained that some Mixed people would naturally gravitate to one side or the other, but that was their choice and needed to be accepted as a natural occurrence.

I shared that some Mixed people wouldn't choose a side—and there was nothing wrong with that either. My heart still stinging from Langston Hughes's poetic betrayal, I cautioned them against perpetuating the "Tragic Mulatto" stereotype. "The only tragedy is the idea that being anything but White makes you inferior," I informed them.

It felt wonderful to get my ideas out of my head and share them with people who listened respectfully. They crowded around and thanked me afterwards. Once I'd tasted that feeling, I no longer wanted to settle for less.

The 1970 Census

In 1970, census questionnaires were mailed to about 70 percent of USA homes, to be completed and mailed back to the census office in their district. Enumerators collected the data in other areas. If a respondent did not fill out "race" on the mailed-in form, an enumerator either visited them and asked them to select from a flashcard showing different racial options, or asked them over the phone. It was assumed that the main respondent's race was the same for other members of the family unless otherwise specified.

People who reported mixed parentage of White and another race were categorized according to the non-White race. Mixed people who weren't mixed with White were categorized by their father's race. This census added "Black" to the Negro category for the first time.

In the "Color or Race" category, respondents were told to fill in one circle for the race they identified most closely with: White, Negro or Black, Indian (Amer.) (with instructions to print the name of their tribe), Japanese, Chinese, Filipino, Hawaiian, Korean, and Other. Korean was added as a category to reflect growing immigration patterns. As in the 1960 census, Mexicans who weren't Indian or another kind of non-White were counted as White.

Thanks to people self-identifying racially, the public was more aware of and vocal about the racial categories, and started demanding that the categories grow to reflect the increasingly diverse USA population, including Southeast Asian refugees from the Vietnam War.

Chapter 20: The Touch of You

Spring fever amped up my unrequited crush on Simon. Though I couldn't deny my attraction to him, I wasn't doing much more than scribbling poems and sending him telepathic messages, still worrying that he thought White girls were the best.

I nearly swooned when, out of the blue, he approached me with his shy smile and asked to walk me to class. Though I had no idea what sparked his sudden interest, I eagerly accepted. Then he invited me to join him for a milkshake after school. Soon, he took me to the movies where he taught me kissing games. This was different than it had been with Ray—Simon's lips and tongue took a confident lead, and mine were eager to follow. He had his own car with a backseat for exploring each other's bodies. To a point. I was a virgin and determined to stay that way. Our budding romance was a sweet relief from the tedium of my classes. I'd wanted him for so long that being in his presence felt like the love songs pouring from the radio.

Then summer came, and Simon went out of town to visit relatives. But my heart was loyal, which meant I wasn't going to a party with Carolyn to check out some fine dude she'd met during summer math class at Franklin High School. But Carolyn begged until we ended up near Rainier Beach in a house full of people we didn't know, trying to act cooler than we were. Red and blue lights cast a sultry glow, cheap wine flowed, and the boys were super fine. The girls were intimidating—their style sharper, their earrings bigger, their makeup bolder. I still hadn't smoked weed, but I recognized the smell, breathing extra deeply in case I could catch a contact high which shouldn't break any laws because hey, I couldn't help it, right?

We danced until our skin glowed under the black lights, every speck of dandruff or lint popping like neon. And somehow in the middle of a slow song by the Dells (or was it the Delfonics?), I found myself in the arms of a muscular, dark-skinned boy with soulful eyes and a hint of danger. He nudged his chin against my ear, breathing words that bypassed my brain and went straight to the trembling between my legs. He drew his lips across the softest part of my neck, then pulled them away, forcing me to arch in his direction asking for more. Though my heart belonged to Simon, my body was succumbing to the music and this stranger's smooth moves.

His lips found mine, and we wound ourselves together 'til I forgot my name in the mix of Kool cigarettes and Doublemint gum that teased my tongue. As Carolyn grabbed my elbow to pull me out the door to make our curfews, he followed, tapping my shoulder.

"I'm Freddy. Let me get that number," he said without a question mark.

I scribbled it inside a matchbook cover, certain he'd never call.

By midsummer, Simon had returned, and we'd fallen into our sweet, familiar pattern. He edged me further with his lips and hands, gentle yet persistent. He didn't need to spell it out; he wanted it all. But I wasn't ready to cross that line. Freddy did call, and I saw him a few times, the rumble of his voice and the growl of his laugh shooting straight to my hormones.

For the rest of the summer, I saw them both, reasoning that since I was still technically a virgin, and neither of them had formally asked me to be their lady, it wasn't cheating. Simon was reliable; Freddy was flaky. Simon was generous; Freddy was greedy. Simon was solid ground; Freddy was a high-wire dance with no net. Simon teased gently, patiently urging me towards the finish line, guiding me with sweet intention. Freddy pushed harder, went further, knew how to leave me in a puddle of yearning. My head and heart battled as both boys enticed me to the outer limits of safe pleasures. Playing with this fire was so delicious that I didn't want to choose. But I knew I could "do it" with just one of them. I had to decide. And the clock was ticking.

Carolyn and Michelle both had steady boyfriends and had finally crossed the line. We giggled over the details, exchanging high-fives. And they asked who I liked best, Simon or Freddy.

"Both of them," I sighed.

"Maybe you could flip a coin," Carolyn laughed.

I worried how I'd choose one over the other, and whether I could live without the two sides of me that they had awakened.

It was August, the time of Seafair, the summer festival that included block parties and parades in different parts of the city. Seafair also brought the Torchlight Parade, the Seafair Cup hydroplane races, and the Blue Angels, an aerobatic team of naval and sometimes other military pilots flying in exciting formations in the skies over Lake Washington.

After Freddy and I watched the Blue Angels, he drove around the South End, cruising slowly around Seward Park as we jammed to Earth, Wind & Fire and War on his radio. He parked and we fell into the back seat where he stole my breath and gave it back in a swirl of minty-menthol heat.

I'd shaved my legs. Twice. And slathered them and the rest of my body in extra lotion. Dabbed some of Mom's cologne on all of my pulse points. Painted my toenails. I wasn't admitting to being ready to go all the way, but I couldn't deny the possibility.

When Freddy's hand moved under my skirt, I pulled away, still not ready to venture into the unknown. He shook his head and mumbled, "you're wearin' me out" as we climbed back into the front seat. Once we left Seward Park, he stopped at a gas station to fill up the car and get cigarettes. My jam came on the radio--Aretha's "Oh Me Oh My, I'm a Fool for You." I closed my eyes to consider which one of my sweethearts I would be a fool for.

Suddenly Freddy's voice floated through the half-open car window. I opened my eyes to see him talking to a guy about his age, who frowned as he looked towards me. I killed the radio and rolled down the window to better hear their conversation.

"You sure, man?" the guy asked, looking skeptical.

"Yeah, man. She's not White. No shit," Freddy said.

"I'm just sayin', I could dig it if you were playin' in the snow, man," his friend chortled.

Freddy shook his head. "She's like half."

His friend looked relieved. "No shit? What's that like?"

"You know, like gettin' two for one." Freddy answered.

"For real?" His friend looked impressed.

"Damn skippy," Freddy laughed loudly, and they slapped five. Twice.

TaRessa Stovall

I rolled up the window and sat up straight. Seconds later, Freddy slid back into the car. "I got you this, sweet thang," he said, handing me a Nestle Crunch bar. My favorite.

"Thanks, "I muttered. She's like half. Two for one. Damn skippy.

He pulled out of the station to turn onto Rainier Avenue. "Just let me out at the bus stop," I said.

He gave me a long sideways look. "Say what?"

"I feel sick," I lied, not sure who I was angrier with—him for his stupid comments, or myself for not having the nerve to confront him.

He moved the car into the right lane, looking confused.

"I think it's my period," I whispered, opening the door at the red light. "Cramps."

Waiting for the bus, I bit into the Nestle Crunch bar. How could I be half and two-for-one at the same time anyway? I tossed the candy into the trash can.

I got off the bus before my house to walk down the hill to Carolyn's house. We called Michelle to meet us there.

"I had to let Freddy go," I said sadly when we'd all gathered.

"What happened?" Michelle asked.

"He got on my nerves." I thought about telling them the whole story, but the hurt was still too raw.

"Besides, I like Simon more. He kisses better too, so—" I managed a wink and a shadow of a smile.

Michelle and Carolyn exchanged a long look.

"What?" I asked.

"I knew you'd pick the light-skinned one," Carolyn sighed.

"No! It's not like that! It's—," I exclaimed

I stood for a full minute, mouth open like a fish dying without water. This wasn't how it was supposed to happen, I thought, reading the skepticism on my friends' faces. Suddenly I was overwhelmed with the futility that came from feeling misunderstood. "You know what? Forget it," I announced, walking away. I bit back tears, stung by my friend's callous assumption. Little did she know that I'd been this close to choosing fiery, flaky Freddy over sweet, steady Simon, until I found out where he was coming from.

I thought of the new song by Curtis Mayfield and the Impressions where they sang about unity between light-skinned and dark-skinned Black people. My favorite line was the one that described the high yella girl as the surface of the deep well of blackness.

I wished Freddy and my friends understood what Curtis was saying. Then I heard rumors that the darker-skinned students in our school's Black Student Union created skits where they cast the lighter-skinned members as White people. This further confirmed the madness of intra-racial divisiveness, which hurt even more than White racism because it cut so much closer to the bone.

Chapter 21: Burn, Baby, Burn!

Near the end of junior year, we studied Shakespeare's "Romeo and Juliet" in English class. The teacher showed the 1968 movie starring Olivia Hussey and Leonard Whiting. But it paled next to the book I was reading, Soledad Brother: The Prison Letters of George Jackson, which included his correspondence to Angela Davis:

> *Dear Angela:*
> *I think about you all of the time ... it gives me occasion for some of the first few really deeply felt ear-to-ear grins. And I've had to increase the number of my daily push-ups by half... I'm not a possessive cat, never demanding, always cool ... I want to hold you (chains and all) and run my tongue in that little gap between your two front teeth ... It's crazy, all women, even the very phenomenal, want at least a promise of brighter days, bright tomorrows. I have no tomorrows at all... You've got it all, African woman. I'm very pleased, if you don't ask me for my left arm, my right eye, both eyes, I'll be very disappointed. You're the most powerful stimulus I could have ... Should we make a lovers' vow? It's silly, with all my tomorrows accounted for, but you can humor me. Power to the People!"* *
>
> **Compiled from selected letters in the book Soledad Brother: The Prison Letters of George Jackson, by George L. Jackson, Bantam Books Inc., 1972*

I found the yearning passion between two brilliant revolutionaries fighting for equality far more captivating than imaginary teens needlessly dying because of crossed signals. The teacher did not appreciate it when I shared this comparison in class.

The more I read about George Jackson and Che Guevara and Fidel Castro and Nat Turner and Harriet Tubman and Frantz Fanon and John Brown and Sojourner Truth—none of it at school, none of it in assigned textbooks—the less I worried about which direction my hair was growing. After learning about Cesar Chavez and the fight to improve the lives of Chicano agricultural workers, I convinced Mom to stop buying iceberg "head" lettuce and green grapes, which had always been staples in our house.

Simon and I were enjoying our pleasure-fueled groove, but the incident with Freddy caused me to backtrack on giving up my virginity. Simon deserved it but as much as I craved him, I wondered if there wasn't something deeper. I wasn't anybody's revolutionary, but I was infatuated with the idea of love fueled by a greater purpose.

Bully's attempts to rile me continued. But they were so lame that I couldn't conjure any real concern, let alone fear that she could actually hurt me.

Maybe it was symbolic that I was reading James Baldwin's The Fire Next Time when she finally upped the ante.

One late spring day, Carolyn and Michelle had stayed after school to check out cheerleading tryouts. I rode the bus alone, devouring Baldwin's wisdom, when I felt a flash of heat at the back of my neck. I shook my head and kept reading. I felt the flash again, closer this time. Seconds later, I felt another flash, and I smelled burnt hair.

"Stop!" the bus supervisor called, rushing over to me. I turned to see Bully holding a lighter near my hair, flicking it on and off. I jumped up to lunge at her, but someone grabbed me from behind and held me back. The bus supervisor stood between us. After asking if I was all right, she marched Bully to the front and ordered her to sit. The bus was uncharacteristically silent.

Now that Bully had raised the stakes, I was ready to respond. After Mom and Greg were asleep, I crept into the kitchen, selecting the biggest knife I could find. I sharpened it, wrapped it carefully in a kitchen towel and slipped it into my purse. This was a new kind of anger for me. It wasn't hot; it was ice-cold. Rather than emotional turmoil, I felt an eerie sense of focused calm.

The next morning at the bus stop, Carolyn and Michelle told me they'd heard what happened. They fussed over me, lifting my hair to check the back of my neck

"I've got somethin' for her ass," I said, fingering the towel that covered the knife in the bottom of my purse. I was finally ready to fight my longtime tormentor, but Bully wasn't on the bus. I looked for her everywhere at school, but couldn't find her. Later that day, Carolyn said she'd heard that Bully had been sent to the psych ward for trying to set my hair on fire. I carried the knife for a few more weeks, in case Carolyn was wrong.

I never saw Bully again. I never learned whether the psych ward rumor was true, but one thing was clear: nobody could beat her ass worse than she was already beating her own.

Chapter 22: Them Changes

The summer of 1971 leading up to my senior year of high school was bittersweet. The country was reeling from the scandal of the Pentagon Papers revealing government secrets behind the Vietnam War. Racial tensions still ran high around the country. When I wasn't working at my summer job through the program for low-income inner-city kids, I was covering my bell-bottom jeans with drawings of peace signs, Black Power fists and the words "Free Love" and "Right On." Michelle and Carolyn teased me about being half Black Power and half Flower Child.

Elmer Dixon, the green-eyed younger co-founder of the Seattle Black Panther Party, had been set up by the police and was serving time in an Oregon prison. If that wasn't depressing enough, on August 21, "Soledad Brother" George Jackson was killed by prison guards in San Quentin. My heart ached for him, for his family, for Angela Davis, and their aborted love. What would the revolution look like now? And why were so many who fought for the people locked up or killed at such a young age?

I found solace and sustenance in the poetic music of a skinny bearded singer named Gil Scott-Heron. His funky, jazzy blues commentaries gave voice to the warrior within me. I played his album, "Pieces of a Man" nonstop. With jams like "Home Is Where the Hatred Is," "Lady Day and John Coltrane," "I Think I'll Call it Morning," and his instant classic, "The Revolution Will Not Be Televised," Gil's fiery music became the drug I needed. It helped me rise each morning and get my mind right to face a world that was making less sense by the day.

I was eager to graduate but unsure what I'd do after that. I still read everything I could get my hands on and filled pages with poems and musings on all the things I yearned to tell the world.

Senior year brought even more change, scattering Michelle, Carolyn and me in different directions. Michelle was pregnant, so she left Roosevelt for a cool inner-city school for teen mothers. Carolyn got serious about college and stopped skipping classes to devote herself to academics. I was drifting, with no goals beyond vague notions of becoming a professional writer of some kind. I had no idea how to make that happen. Nobody had ever mentioned the possibility of college to me, and I didn't see any point in pursuing that road.

Michelle had a darling baby girl and impressed us all—including herself—by swiftly maturing into a responsible grown-up and doting mother.

After graduation, I relied on my typing skills to get an office job working at an educational non-profit organization. Carolyn was accepted into the University of Washington, and we found an apartment together behind Meany Middle School.

I raced through all of my clerical work, then used the IBM Selectric typewriter to pound out long, semi-coherent rants about being Mixed and wanting the world to meet me on my own terms. My boss, a young, dynamic Black man named Tommy "T.J." Vassar, didn't seem bothered as long as I finished my real work first.

The chair of the board of directors of our non-profit was a serious, bespectacled young man named Larry Gossett. He'd been an activist with the Dixon brothers and moved on to recruiting students of color whose parents hadn't attended college to the University of Washington. Larry would talk with me before meeting with T.J. "Why aren't you in college?" he'd always ask.

I explained that I didn't need school to be a writer.

"What do you write?"

"Mostly things about being Mulatto," I said proudly.

"Mulatto?" He looked surprised. "That's what you call yourself?"

"That's what I am."

"Are you non-White?"

"Yes."

"Are you non-Black?"

"No."

"Then you're Black." We argued passionately, and I started looking forward to our debates. Larry always finished by saying, "You've got to stop wasting your brain and go to school." I protested that college couldn't teach me anything I didn't already know.

One day Larry issued a challenge. "What if I told you that I could get you into the university?" When I protested that my low high school GPA and lack of money would make it impossible, he told me not to worry. "You're smart and you have a lot to say. Tell you what—just fill out the papers, and we'll see what happens."

I couldn't believe it when I was admitted to the University of Washington. Larry had been right. Carolyn squealed with joy when I showed her the paperwork. "What do you want to study?" I couldn't answer, still trying to comprehend the enormity of this miracle.

We were deep into the era of Blaxploitation movies, action films aimed at Black audiences, some with anti-establishment plots. Early hits in this new genre included "Sweet Sweetback's Baadasssss Song," "Shaft," "Cotton Comes to Harlem," "The Mack" and "Cool Breeze." While some of these movies were criticized for having stereotypical characters and glorifying violence, it was exciting to see entertainment for, by and about Black people on the big screen. My mind was blown by a scene in the film "Superfly," the story of a drug dealer who creates a risky scheme to move enough cocaine to escape his dangerous hustle.

Curtis Mayfield's soundtrack was the best part of the movie. My mind was blown by a montage cut to the beat of the music that showed the characters using cocaine. That scene hypnotized me, proving how seductive film could be. When a well-known activist-around-town straightened his signature Afro and started wearing flashy bell-bottoms, long leather coats, and showy platform shoes to look like the lead character in "Superfly," I recognized the power of film to change people's behavior. Considering my miraculous admission to the University, learning to make movies didn't feel like such an impossible dream.

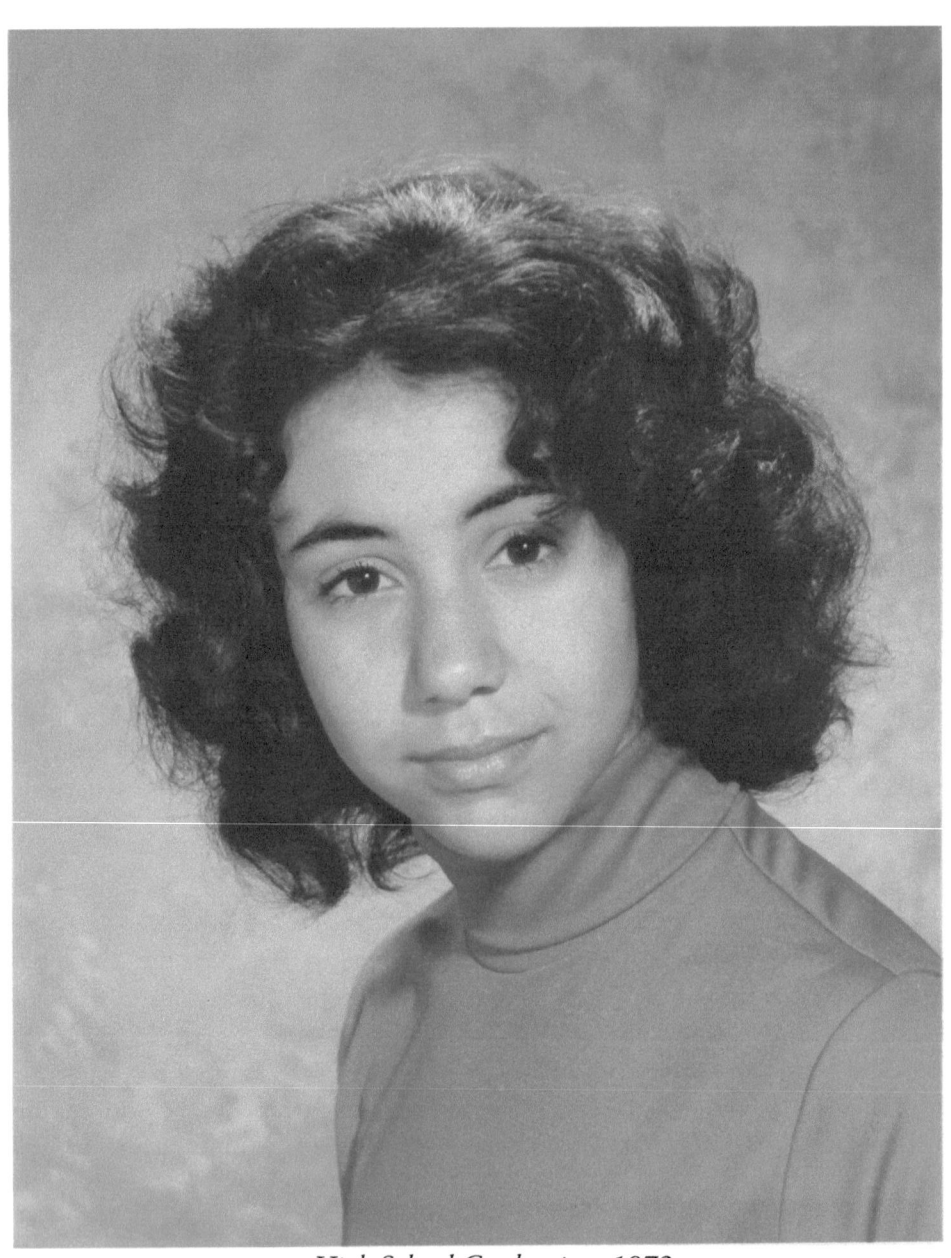
High School Graduation, 1972

Chapter 23: Blow Hair

I kept pinching myself, unable to believe I was a full-fledged college student—the first in my family. Once I got my schedule together, I met with my guidance counselor, a laid-back brother with an encouraging personality. "Do you know what you want to major in?"

"Film and television," I said confidently.

"I think you'll do very well," he said. "But there's one thing I don't understand: Where it says 'race' you wrote 'Mulatto'"--

"That's what I am."

"Right," he said, "except there's nothing like that in the Office of Minority Affairs. Your financial aid is here, in the Black department." He picked up his pen to change the form.

"Wait!" I cried. "I want all of my identity to be represented, including my mother."

He set the pen on his desk, looking at me like I was crazy. I could see and feel him reaching deep to summon the patience he needed to persuade me. "I hear you. But you won't get your financial aid unless it says 'Black' on that line. I'm not saying you're not proud of your background or that you need to ignore either of your parents. We just don't have a separate category or a separate office. Your money is Black."

"If I don't have a choice—" I conceded reluctantly. He nodded, looking relieved. I made the correction. He signed the completed forms and sent me downstairs to the cashier's window.

I felt like a sellout. After an hour in the financial aid line, I stood in front of an older Black woman who looked from me to the scratched out "Mulatto" replaced by "Black" a few times. I read the questions in her eyes. This wouldn't be happening if they'd let me keep "Mulatto" on there, I thought. Mumbling under her breath, she finally handed me my Black money. My college career was officially underway.

Speaking of Black, I was thrilled to be taking my first Afro-American literature course with Professor M. I'd never had a Black teacher before. She was slender, her beauty softening with age, with straightened hair in a short bob that framed her large, expressive eyes.

I had never heard of Zora Neale Hurston, the author of the first book assigned in Professor M's course. From page one, Their Eyes Were Watching God, grabbed me by the heart and wouldn't let go.

Little did I know what the professor had in mind. The second week of class, she stood in front of me. I looked up, smiling expectantly, visions of the Panther Party's Political Education classes dancing in my head.

"This," she announced loudly, pointing a manicured nail at my head, "is what we call 'blow hair.'" She looked around the room, then back at me. "Do you know what that means?"

I shook my head, cheeks burning.

"Well!" she said, turning to the class triumphantly. "It means hair that moves in the wind and conveys a certain way of being."

I bit back the curses that rose in my throat and resisted the urge to ask the professor why she straightened her hair instead of sporting a Black-is-Beautiful Afro. Only the intoxicating brilliance of Zora Neale Hurston's writing kept me from dropping that class. I was too in love with the enticing tale of Janie to deprive myself of that magnificent book. But I couldn't sleep until I shared my thoughts with Professor M for the way she had singled me out.

I wrote her a letter, pouring my anger onto the typewriter keys. I described the sadistic White woman teacher I'd had in fourth and fifth grades who humiliated me by sitting me in front of the classroom to cut my bangs while she ridiculed my hair texture. I told the tale of the neighborhood girls who'd driven me to cut off all my hair with their predictions that it would make me stuck up. I detailed the time Aunt Shirley had forced a haircut on me one Minneapolis summer before Mom arrived to take us home. I broke down

Stella's obsession and fiery attack. I explained how all my life I'd heard about "good" hair and "bad" hair, but that her attempt to single me out as an example of "blow" hair just didn't make any sense. I concluded by saying that if she were going to try to make an example of my hair, she needed to understand more of its history before making assumptions.

After class, I handed the professor my letter. "You need to read this."

"I'm sorry," she said haughtily. "I don't give extra credit."

"I'm not looking for any credit," I said, holding it in her face until she took it. I don't know if she read what I wrote. She didn't acknowledge it, but I figured the least I could do was express where I was coming from. Maybe then she wouldn't ridicule any more of her students.

The next book we studied in Professor M's class was *The Bluest Eye* by Toni Morrison. Where Zora Neal Hurston's language had seduced me into a state of infatuation, Toni Morrison's searing depiction of Pecola, a dark-skinned girl who craved the balm of whiteness to cope with the pain she suffered from a color-struck society was like a one-two punch to my gut and my head. Once I recovered enough to process the story, *The Bluest Eye* helped me better understand the monster of color-struck madness and gave voice to the pain and confusion it caused for so many people.

I flashed back to when I was six years old and my friend Sheryl came to our house to play with some old makeup that Mom had given us. We sat on our sun-dappled back porch in front of Mom's special lighted portable mirror, decorating our eyes, lips and cheeks with bright colors.

"You look so pretty!" I told Sheryl, marveling at how her natural beauty shone through the shades that were made for my mother's freckled Jewish skin.

She frowned at me. "No! You're the pretty one," she insisted. I was surprised at the intensity of her response.

"Nuh uh," I argued, reasoning that anyone with eyeballs could see that Sheryl's features were much lovelier than mine, even covered in garish streaks of makeup.

She shook her head, lips pursed tightly. That's when I saw how my heartfelt compliments felt like mockery in a world that couldn't see beauty across the color spectrum.

We rushed to the bathroom, scrubbed the makeup from our faces, and then ran outside to find our other friends and play games that didn't force us to confront issues we weren't ready to fully understand.

I felt that same gnawing in my gut whenever Black adults gushed about how pretty I was. Their overly lavish praise bothered me in ways I couldn't articulate and never knew how to respond to. Toni Morrison gave me language in her heart-rending tale of Pecola's struggle to survive the madness of people who were color-blinded—not blind to color, but rendered sightless by it until they were unable to view the full human living within the covering we call skin.

I wondered whether there was a connection between Pecola's name and that of the tragic Mulatto Peola in the dreaded "Imitation of Life" book and film. In an interview, Toni Morrison explained that she wanted to take Peola's name and "play with it, turn it around" for The Bluest Eye.

I didn't know who was more obsessed with this color thing—me or the rest of the world. But I was grateful to Toni Morrison for placing it front and center in such a powerful way. It reminded me how books had the power to make sense of chaos and insanity.

Chapter 24: When the Revolution Comes

Several students invited me to join the university's Black Student Union. Remembering how Bully had banished me from my high school BSU, I chuckled at the irony of being sought after for membership. I even considered joining. But before I could decide, Larry Gossett told me about a group called the Third World Coalition that sounded intriguing. It brought together Black, Asian, Latino, Native American and a few ethnically ambiguous-looking people from different countries and cultures, with a shared passion for changing the world through progressive politics. The Third World Coalition was more captivating than most of my classes, with passionate discussions about culture, politics and the many dimensions of revolution, televised and otherwise. We dissected television shows, music, movies, books—and shared aspects of our various cultures. I was hungry to learn more about other groups and the larger world. The conversations were more like the political education classes back at the Black Panther house. I was intoxicated by learning about different topics from so many varied perspectives, with a global twist. Nobody flinched or corrected me when I said I was Mulatto. And nobody suggested that I had no right to be in the room.

    A handsome Chinese guy who shared some provocative ideas in the Coalition meetings started talking to me. Soon, he'd asked for my number, given me a ride home, and invited me to a jazz concert. I'd never dated an Asian guy or been to a jazz concert, but as my awareness of the world expanded, I was ready to grow.

    I'd been to plenty of R&B concerts, but never anything so grown-up where we sat politely in dressy clothes waiting for the artist to appear. I was excited about my date with this new guy, and about this new musical experience.

TaRessa Stovall

Shortly after we took our seats, a Black couple sat in the row ahead of us. The woman had a big Afro, but I could still see the stage. "Her hair is so gross," my date said.

"Say what?" I hoped I'd heard wrong.

"Her hair," He gestured towards it with a goofy smile. "It's so ugly. I'm glad yours isn't like that. Aren't you?"

I knew he'd spent money on our tickets. I was torn—should I sit silently and ignore his insult? Wait until later to confront him? Or split? As the lights dimmed to signal the start of the show. I grabbed my purse, stood up and walked out, ignoring his voice calling after me.

I walked the long way home, cursing the whole time. Was everybody racist and obsessed with different kinds of hair? Why had he thought I'd agree with his funky attitude?

The next day, a Black guy who was in one of my classes walked up to me as I was crossing the quad. Other than a quick "hey," we'd never spoken before. "Um sister, can I rap with you for a moment? Please?"

I halted, surprised. "What's happenin'?"

His demeanor was stiff, his face serious, and his voice stern. "Well, sister, I've seen you walking around campus with that Oriental guy—"

"Asian. Chinese. American-born."

"Yeah well uh, you know, I just wondered why you're with him. Why you never gave a brother a chance. You know we've got to stick together around here."

"I'm not dating him," I said. "But why do you care anyway? You don't know me, but now you want to be all up in my business?"

"I'm just saying, give us brothers a chance." He smiled, as if that would help.

"So, all you Black guys dating White or Asian, Samoan or Chicana women—why is it okay for you but not for us?" I asked.

"Not me, sister. I just don't like seeing a Black queen like yourself— "

"You know I'm Mixed, right?"

"Oh, you're one of those confused— "

"You're the one who's confused, brother. You need to get yourself together," I said, flashing a fake smile as I walked away.

Days later, I saw the same guy macking on a blonde White woman. I laughed loudly enough for him to look at me. I caught his gaze and shook my head slowly until he looked away. The next semester, I had my first Afro-American history course with Dr. JC, a very tall, rotund Black man who referred to White people as Germans. When asked why, he gave a rambling lecture on the origins of White people being Germanic or something like that. Later, I heard Black students saying that his marriage to a White woman made him a hypocrite and invalidated everything he was teaching. "He talks Black, but sleeps White," was the frequent criticism. This was one of many conversations I heard on campus and in the community about whether a Black person could love or marry a White person and still be down for the people, committed to the cause. I added that to the seemingly endless list of questions for which I had no answers.

Chapter 25: Twilight Child

One leader of the Third World Coalition was Rhonda Oden, a charismatic Creole girl with a passion for progressive politics. She spoke softly but eloquently about justice, equality, and building solidarity to work for change.

When Rhonda said that she was publishing an anthology of writing from Coalition members, I asked what she was looking for.

"Something dynamic, something that represents you," she said with an encouraging smile.

I could barely wait to start writing. The words flew onto the paper as if they'd been building up my whole life:

TWILIGHT CHILD

Twilight Child.
Too this to be that
And too that to be this.
WHAT ARE YOU?
When I was 4, I said:
"I'm Mixed."
When I was 14, I said:
"I'm Black."
Now,
I say "Mulatto"—
A castrated term
Dug out of a mildewed history
In a desperate attempt
To find a label that fit well,
Was the right color, and did not say
DRY CLEAN ONLY.

Mulatto changed from a label
To a weapon—
I aimed it at the world
With a hatred borne
Of years of watching
And waiting
For them to stop asking me:
WHAT ARE YOU???
You're Black, are you White, you look White,
you act Black…
You seem to be,
You ought to be,
You've got to be…
A Twilight Child.

They call me nigger and high yella and half-breed…
And I call them fools.
They throw their insecurities at me
And then tell me not to be hung up,
Not to think or talk or write so much
About what I am.

TaRessa Stovall

*For 19 years, I've listened to their (his-) stories
And when I try to tell mine, they run away—
Afraid to look into my paradoxical world,
Scared that the mirror of my soul will tell them
That they are NOT the fairest of them all.*

*They ask me to justify classifying myself "Mulatto"
Black folks wanna know where I get off at acknowledging being a half-breed
And White folks resent the fact that I never have and never will
Feel inferior to them—no, not to them, or anyone else:
And never having felt inferior, I have no reason
To pretend superiority.
And while they look on my differences with fear and distrust,
I am confident that I can survive in my Twilight world as well as, if not better
than they do in theirs.
I'm oh-so-hip to them, and have mastered the art
Of getting over in this continually alien environment.*

*Twilight Children HAVE to be strong;
There is no rest for those who want to be proud.
And so I have to deal with myself, for myself, by myself;
I have to find myself, and then protect what I have found
For it will certainly be under attack.*

*RACE—Check one:
White
Black
Oriental
American Indian
Spanish Sur-name*

Other

Black/White

White/Black

other

Other

OTHER.

Copyright TaRessa Stone, 1973

I'd never been so scared to show anyone a poem before. This was the rawest, most naked thing I'd ever written. I didn't think anybody was ready for this level of truth.

Once I handed my masterpiece to Rhonda, I lost sleep worrying about whether I'd be criticized, ostracized, thrown out of the Third World Coalition for being too confrontational. I was one big knot of anxiety until Rhonda threw her arm over my shoulder, and told me how much she liked the poem.

"Really?" I squeaked, struggling to breathe.

"Hell, yes! It's in-your-face and powerful."

I hugged her gratefully and floated on air for a few hours. Then I started worrying about how other people would react. I considered skipping classes, or coming to campus in disguise. I was shocked when other poets from the anthology congratulated me. Some even said that my poem would help them to see Mixed people differently. Classmates I'd never really spoken to thanked me for opening their minds. I was euphoric. There was nothing better than feeling like my words could reach people and help us all understand each other a little better.

Chapter 26: True Grits

I finished my first year at the University of Washington with flying colors. By year two, I was impatient to learn about film and television. My first communications course started with the professor insisting that actual hands-on work experience meant more than academics when it came to working in the media. He emphasized that if we wanted to get into the industry, even an unpaid internship or sweeping the floors was better than a degree. I sat up and took note.

Life was about to lead me to a whole 'nother kind of experience. My new Political Science professor—a young Italian man notorious for his radical politics—kicked off the semester by letting us choose between coming to class and taking tests and volunteering "to do something useful in the community." Leaving class, I ran into Elmer Dixon, who was on campus collecting donations for the Black Panthers' Free Breakfast Program. I asked him about doing some volunteer work with the Panther Party for my Political Science credit.

"We could use your help with the Free Breakfast Program," he said.

"Sounds great!" I said, "Sign me up."

"You have to get up at five in the morning and cook for a bunch of kids," he said, regarding me skeptically.

"I can do that," I said confidently, though I'd never done either of those things in my life.

We exchanged phone numbers and I gave Elmer my address, where a van would pick me up before sunrise the next day.

I barely slept, terrified that I'd miss the 4:30 a.m. alarm. Bleary-eyed, I showered, dressed and ran downstairs to meet the Panther van, fighting to keep my eyes open. Elmer was as jovial and energetic as ever.

While beautiful children in all shades of brown filled the tables, Elmer taught me to cook grits, which I'd never even tasted before. "Make sure they don't have lumps. These kids will talk about you if your food is nasty."

I stirred the grits as if my life depended on it, smushing anything that threatened to turn into a lump. I measured the salt and pepper exactly as Elmer showed me, and was relieved when none of the children complained. By the time we'd fed them all and cleaned up, I was ready for a nap. But I jumped in the van and went back to school, high on the feeling of making a tangible difference.

The next day, Elmer taught me how to make French toast. While we were cleaning up afterwards, a Black woman volunteer who was a few years older than me asked the familiar question: What are you?

I'd started asking people to guess, to see what they came up with. Common assumptions were Chicana, Samoan, Asian, and Native American. Nobody ever guessed correctly. Lack of sleep made me short on words, so I just mumbled, "Mixed."

"With what?"

"My mama and my daddy," I retorted, grabbing a broom to sweep the littered floor.

"But what are you?"

I considered reciting my "Twilight Child" poem. My soul sagged with the weariness of this endless identity dance. Of being pushed to explain my existence. Of not being trusted until I passed whatever test any random person felt like administering.

I wanted the answer that shut the questions down. Exhaling my frustration, I muttered, "Black. And Jewish."

"But what are you?" she asked.

"I just told you," I said through clenched teeth.

"No. What are you?"

We went through several more rounds of her asking the same question. She kept going, no matter what I answered. After I'd run through all that I knew of all four of my grandparents' origins, I threw up my hands and stopped responding. But her question hung in the air.

That night, a lightbulb went on in my head.

The next morning, I got right in her face and said, "I'm Black."

"Right on," she said with an approving smile. I wasn't sure whether I'd sold out or just faced the truth of my reality. But I regretted the countless times I'd detailed my ancestral background to people when all they really wanted to know was whose back I'd have when the shit went down.

Chapter 27: Starstruck

I loved college and certainly never planned to drop out. But when a television job became available, I followed my communications professor's advice and became a production assistant on a Black history television documentary on the other side of Washington state. Mom wasn't thrilled, but she managed to seem supportive.

In that job, I got the hands-on experience I craved, doing everything from typing script changes on different-colored paper, to organizing shooting logistics, setting up and tearing down camera equipment, and running errands for anyone who asked.

It was cool until the boss started sexually harassing me. Soon, I was back in Seattle where I lived with Mom and worked temporary odd jobs. Still determined to keep learning the business, I found two mentors at the local network television stations. Bill Dorsey and Andy Reynolds were wise, nurturing, non-harassing Black men who taught me the ropes and let me tag along on their news assignments.

Little did I know I was about to discover the most mesmerizing Black writer of my generation. This was 1975, when a phenomenon called for colored girls who have considered suicide/when the rainbow is enuf, took the world by storm. It was wrapped in a new art form called "choreopoetry" that set the New York theatre world on fire. The fiery writing of a young poet named Ntozake Shange was combined with music, movement and drama to express the lives and loves of a bouquet of Black women identified only by the colors they wore: Lady in Red, Lady in Blue, Lady in Orange, etc.

I devoured the book version of for colored girls, instantly strung out on the sheer force and musicality of the language: jazzy, bluesy, ancient and futuristic. Ntozake (Xhosa for "she who has her own things") Shange (Zulu for "he/she who walks/lives with lions") conjured some life-changing magic with her wordplay. I strutted around my room reading the poems aloud, wishing more than anything that I could see the full choreopoem onstage. While I didn't understand all of the references to New York City Black/Latino culture sprinkled throughout, every syllable reverberated in my soul. I found pieces of my story in hers, and hers in mine.

As I toiled away at my generic office job, I started forming an idea for a screenplay. At the university, I became friends with a glamorous, statuesque light-skinned woman named Yolaine Vallot. I asked if she was related to Johnny Vallot, my high school friend from the basketball team.

"He is my brother. But our name is pronounced Val-low, not Val-lot," she said, visibly annoyed. "We are Creoles."

I'd admired Yolaine's passionate writing in the Third World Coalition anthology that Rhonda had compiled. At first, I was intimidated by her striking beauty and confident charisma. But we made each other laugh, loved debating politics and the Revolution, and shared a love of good food and a passion to change the world through our writing.

While Yolaine studied journalism at the UW, I was back to working a boring office job, obsessed with finding a way to express my creativity. She turned me onto some great movies including "The Harder They Come" from Jamaica, and "Black Orpheus" from Brazil. Inspired, I convinced her to help me write a screenplay, a Black love story with a twist: a dark-skinned woman as the romantic lead. This went against the grain at a time when light-skinned, long-haired beauty Jayne Kennedy was the standard sister sex symbol. I wasn't sure America was ready for its color-struck culture to be challenged, but I was determined to try.

Yolaine and I drafted the synopsis, fleshing out the characters and their romantic drama, weaving in references to community activism and power to the people, right on. With the naivete of youth, we envisioned the stunning Cicely Tyson for the lead and wholesomely sultry Jayne Kennedy for her sidekick. We wanted Michael Schultz, the Black director who'd helmed my favorite coming-of-age drama, "Cooley High," and the hit comedy, "Car Wash," to direct.

When my bosses at work looked the other way, I surreptitiously made long distance calls to find out how to contact these superstars, with no luck.

Then Yolaine and I heard that Cicely Tyson was substituting for Mia Farrow in a live performance of "Joan of Arc" in Seattle. We agreed that Yolaine—being the bolder one with media connections—would get a press pass, and find a way to get backstage to ask Ms. Tyson to consider our project.

Yolaine got the press pass—then came down with a stomach bug. "You have to go in my place," she insisted. I was terrified, but knew it was our best and probably only chance to get anywhere near Cicely Tyson in the flesh. We banked on the fact that our similar coloring would fool security into letting me in with Yolaine's press pass.

With our precious film presentation in a blue notebook tucked under my arm, I smiled and flirted with the security guard until he grudgingly let me in. Once Ms. Tyson was onstage, I sneaked backstage, found her dressing room, and climbed into the large wooden armoire near her dressing table. I scrunched down, careful not to squish the notebook, praying that I wouldn't be discovered before she finished her performance.

Finally, the show ended, and the great Ms. Cicely Tyson was escorted back to her dressing room. I heard the door close and climbed out of the armoire on unsteady legs, startling the gorgeous star as she sat at her makeup table.

Starstruck by her radiant presence, I babbled an introduction and handed her the package. She accepted it graciously, regarding me with wide eyes that veered between frightened and bemused. "So, if you'll look it over and let us know—" I said breathlessly...

A hefty security guard materialized to drag me from the room. "We'd really appreciate it, Ms. Tyson! You're our favorite!" I called happily over my shoulder.

She must have taken us seriously, because a few weeks later, her agency sent us a letter saying they might be interested, based on the finished screenplay. Jayne Kennedy's agent sent a similar letter. We jumped for joy, certain we were headed for the big time. Yolaine and I roughed out the rest of the script, then traveled to Los Angeles to meet with industry bigwigs. We called and wrote to several, but the only one who granted us a meeting was a Jewish studio executive who seemed intrigued by our moxie and impressed by the fact that we'd gotten responses from Cicely Tyson and Jayne Kennedy.

His advice wasn't what we expected. "It's almost impossible for first-timers like yourselves, unknowns, to get a screenplay produced. You should write the story as a novel and get it published first. Then you have a better chance of

Hollywood showing some interest."

He knocked the wind right out of our rookie sails. Unsure what to do next, we put our passion project on hold while life took us in different directions. Yolaine joined a prestigious journalism training program in California, and I did some traveling. I still wanted to create stories that defied stereotypes, but didn't have a clue how to make that happen.

As I was trying to get my professional goals together, my baby brother taught me new ways to think about how racial identity and culture intersected. Greg came to me for advice: some kids at school had invited him to go on a skiing trip. What should he do?

I didn't even have to think about it. "You can't go! "I said in my bossy, big sister voice.

"Why not," he said, looking at me like I was crazy.

"Black people don't ski," I proclaimed.

"Who says?" he countered.

"We just don't." I didn't know where that idea came from, but it popped out of my mouth like the undisputed gospel truth straight from the tablet of Moses. Fortunately, Greg ignored me and had a great time skiing.

I didn't agree with my parents that aligning myself with Blackness would hold me back or limit my options. But I was starting to understand how some popular notions of Black identity weren't always as etched in stone as I'd been told. It made sense that just a few years after Jim Crow ended in the South—and its more subtle northern spin-offs were beginning to fall out of favor—Black America was working overtime to define itself. As terminology shifted from Colored to Negro to Black and proud, popular notions of what constituted identity were in flux.

I'd become aware of skiing as a popular pastime in high school, where many White classmates spent weekends racing down snowy mountain slopes. They came back with deep suntans even in the dead of winter. Many times, they sported casts on arms and legs broken on the slopes like badges of pride. One thing was clear: skiing was for people with money. Plus, the idea of voluntarily spending hours frolicking outside in snowy weather while risking broken bones was not generally considered appealing to the Black people in my world.

At first, I worried that Greg was losing touch with his Black side. I watched him carefully, alert for warning signs that he'd fallen into the trap of denial. The more I saw, I realized that Greg was not allowing anyone's limited ideas to keep him from trying something new. I admired him for being grounded in the reality of his background while not letting anyone restrict his sense of identity or the way he moved through the world.

We laughed about the fact that while I was adamant about telling people exactly what I was each and every time, he was comfortable being more strategic. Greg was much better at reading people and situations than I was, and he sometimes let people think whatever they wanted about his background and identity, and then used their assumptions to his advantage. As he grew into a young man, I noticed that while he moved with quiet confidence among people of different races, he was very drawn to the Asian culture around us. Seattle is the closest city to Asia on the U.S. mainland. While Hawaii is closer and has a higher Asian population, Seattle serves as a major port for Asian business.

Unlike me, Greg was not forced to integrate high school. He got to attend Franklin, the coolest multiracial high school in the city. There, he hung out with kids of all races and discovered an affinity for the cultures of his Chinese, Japanese, Filipino and Korean friends.

Greg studied martial arts with a protégée of superstar Bruce Lee, where he internalized the discipline and spiritual philosophies of the art forms. He didn't deny any of his heritage, and he wasn't trying to be something he wasn't. He just followed his natural interests and the culture that spoke to his soul.

That made me wonder: if people like LeAnn and Bully's passing cousin could lean naturally toward their White ancestry, and people like Celia and me leaned toward our Black ancestry, why couldn't a Mixed person feel a strong connection to a people and culture that weren't part of his or her bloodline? By living his truth, my baby brother challenged me to consider a wider range of possibilities.

TaRessa Stovall

A drawing of me for my first book, Soulsong, a self-published collection of my poetry.

Chapter 28: Alla My Stuff

I was twenty-one when mom's younger sister, Aunt Shirley, invited me to see New York City for the first time. She'd divorced Uncle Meyer and left Minneapolis to marry a wealthy Jewish businessman on the east coast. I eagerly accepted her invitation, visions of finally seeing *"For Colored Girls"* —my first real Broadway show—dancing in my mind.

    I almost didn't recognize my auntie. She'd transformed from a drab, middle-class Midwestern suburban housewife to a glamorous wealthy woman draped in expensive clothing and jewels. Even her subtle cologne conveyed the luxe life as she casually ordered the best of everything.

    I soaked it in, wide-eyed, as private drivers whisked us from one place to the next. My senses worked overtime to process the onslaught of color, sound and energy. I was mesmerized by the spectrum of people I saw—all hues intermingled in this hyperactive space. So many of them looked like me, and vice-versa.

    Auntie Shirley wanted me to see high-class New York City. We stayed in a fancy hotel, ate at exclusive restaurants, and visited ritzy tourist spots. It was amazing, but I longed to see Harlem, to taste the city's many flavors on a level I could relate to. I wanted to mingle with the people. Instead, she dragged me to Tiffany's and got mad when I refused to let her buy me a diamond trinket because I wasn't comfortable with the politics of the diamond trade.

    I was relieved when she said she'd gotten tickets for a Broadway show. "I think you'll like it. It's colored," she said.

    "Yes! You mean *For Colored Girls*? I asked breathlessly.

"Oh no," she frowned. "Porgy and Bess."

I shook my head so hard I almost became dizzy. "Aunt Shirley, I know that's a classic, but there's this new play, *"For Colored Girls"*…"—

"So I've heard," she scoffed. "It sounds atrocious."

"But I have to see it," I cried." You don't understand. It's—"

"It's your first time in New York. You need to see some real art," she commanded.

I swallowed, trying not to curse or cry out that I had no interest in that old-timey foolishness written by a White man. Porgy and Bess was gorgeously produced and full of amazing talent, but I just glared at the stage, trying to call up the words to for colored girls… in my head. My heart broke knowing I'd never see it with my own eyes, hear it with my own ears, though it was playing not far away.

While I was processing my anger and sadness about that missed opportunity, Auntie Shirley dropped an even bigger bomb as we were about to check out of the hotel. "I can't believe it, but it turns out I was wrong."

"Wrong? About what?" I asked.

"You can't pass for White. Every colored person we passed looked at you, as if they recognized something in you. Didn't you notice?" she asked, as if her question made any kind of sense.

I stared at her, dumbstruck. "Am I some kind of crazy research project to you?"

She shook her head, ignoring my question. "I owe your mother an apology. I always thought it would be better if you passed for White." She sighed. "Now I see that's not possible."

"Thank you for the visit to New York," I said coldly, stepping back when she tried to hug me. I cried all the way to the airport and through the cross-country flight, both for her betrayal and for missing for colored girls…

When we were children, Mom sent Greg and me to Minneapolis for a few weeks each summer. Our visit with Auntie Shirley and Uncle Mike gave Mom a brief respite from the rigors of single parenting and working around the clock.

Unlike most of the Jewish people who moved from North Minneapolis to the suburb of St. Louis Park, Auntie Shirley wanted a less ethnic environment. She persuaded her very Jewish husband Uncle Meyer to get a fancy ranch house in Golden Valley, which was mostly White. And like Seattle, White in the Twin Cities often meant Scandinavian.

It was like being transported to a different planet. While their home was much larger than ours, Auntie Shirley had plastic covers on her living room furniture, with strict orders never to go into the room unless we were invited or had permission. They didn't have children, and Auntie Shirley was more cerebral than maternal. Her cooking was bland compared to Mom's, and she was finicky about everything, including this new thing called air conditioning. As hot as it got while we were there, she never wanted to turn it on until sweat was dripping down our faces.

There was so little color in the population of Golden Valley that Greg and I didn't attract much attention. When we first arrived, our skin was pale. The Minnesota sun and trips to swim the various lakes soon gave us more color, but the usual curiosity and racial vibes were absent. Our aunt and uncle gave us bikes, which we rode around the suburb, marveling at the strange environment with no sidewalks. Our favorite destination was a strip mall, with a drugstore that sold an exotic drink called Cherry Coke. Sometimes when we pedaled up there, we saw construction workers with Brown and Black faces. They checked us out, sometimes waving in recognition. Even when we got caught shoplifting in the drugstore, there were no racial undertones. The store manager scolded us sternly, made us give everything back, and told us to go home.

Greg looked at me and asked, "Is this what it feels like to be White?" I shrugged. "I guess so." I knew what he meant. In that sterile environment, I felt untethered, suspended from reality. There was nothing in Golden Valley to ground me. Then Mom would fly out to join us, and we'd make at least one visit to a Mixed Jazz Baby family in North Minneapolis, where I regained my sense of balance and felt the color seep back into my being.

As the most ethnic-looking of all her siblings, I guess Auntie Shirley had been running towards Whiteness all her life. Though I was still angry at her, I understood why she'd been obsessed with trying to smash me into that mold—she'd probably longed to pass. I felt sorry for her. But I could never forgive her for trying to cram me into her unfulfilled fantasies or making me miss the original Broadway production of for colored girls… in all its shimmering, bodacious, multi-colored glory.

Chapter 29: Mixed Madness

After my New York misadventure, I was back at the University of Washington to finish my second year. I was four years older than when I'd left, a bit more mature, and determined to get serious about writing and learning to make films.

I'd put my interest in Mixed identity on the back burner. Then Mom handed me a newspaper article about a group called the Citizens for Classification of Interracial Children (CCIC) who were fighting to get an "interracial" category on the 1980 Census, which was three years away.

The leader of CCIC was a White woman who was frustrated by the lack of a category for when trying to transfer her 10-year-old son from one Seattle school to another. Remembering my struggles to have "Mulatto" recognized on my college paperwork, I joined the CCIC, excited about the opportunity for Mixed people to finally be acknowledged and counted.

Jet magazine came to Seattle to write about the CCIC's efforts. Titled "Seattle's Interracial Children, A Question of Choice and Pride," it featured my "Mama, What's a Nigger?" poem I'd written after Dr. King's murder along with a picture of Greg and me sitting on Mom's front porch and a description of my drama with trying to claim "Mulatto" on my college financial aid forms.

I attended the CCIC meetings, eager to share my thoughts and experiences. But I noticed a troubling pattern: when myself and other Mixed people tried to speak up, we were ignored or talked over by the parents of Mixed kids. I didn't want to admit it, but they acted like our voices didn't count.

As much as I craved a category that didn't force us to choose sides or chop ourselves into racial fractions, I worried that these parents wanted a Mixed classification so their kids wouldn't be considered "merely" Black. While I still wanted to fight for a new census designation to accurately represent my whole reality and family and better explain me to the world, I had serious doubts that the CCIC was the best pathway to that goal. I drifted away from the organization, tucking my militant Mixed dreams into the back of my mind.

Another troubling pattern was emerging. Suddenly, a stream of guys—some who I'd dated, others I'd had crushes on, and a few who were just plain friends—felt compelled to confide in me that they were dating White women. And they didn't just mention it casually in the midst of everyday conversations. They sought me out specifically to drop this bomb, with the headline, "I have something important to tell you."

They breathlessly shared this information as though I alone could grant them some official permission. Their voices were drowned out by memories of the male voices of my youth insisting that "White girls are better than you because…" These memories made their choices and confessions feel more personal than they probably were. As their eyes begged for my seal of approval, I blinked back tears and told them how happy I was that they'd found what they were looking for.

Despite all the years of hearing Black boys and men claim that White girls and women epitomized everything they wanted, I never felt inferior to those women. Maybe I'd been immunized by society and media relentlessly promoting White superiority in all forms. Instead, I was sad and sometimes angry at how easily so many guys had fallen for the brainwashing. Whatever their motives, I wished they'd leave me out of their decisions to cross the color line. I despised feeling torn between the idea that I was co-signing their rejection of Black women and being expected to celebrate every Mixed couple because they might produce a kid like me.

Occasionally, I'd meet a White woman who shared her desire to date a Black man and "have a beautiful Mixed baby." They waited, expectantly, for my verdict. I just rolled my eyes and left the conversations, hating the idea that they'd create a child under those circumstances.

Maybe those men and women who sought my Mixed blessing viewed me as a safe haven, assuming I'd happily sanction their choices. Perhaps they hoped my approval would shield them from the criticism and judgment of others. Or that I automatically celebrated every Mixed couple because they symbolized my origins.

Mixed couples were never as interesting to me as Mixed children. But when I did think about the couples, I divided them into two categories. There were the ones who genuinely loved their partners and embraced the partner's as part of that love. As long as their priority was the person and not their color, I was cool with them. I didn't like the ones who boasted a preference for the other race, and/or had a policy against dating their own kind, especially when they made a point of talking badly about people like themselves. They got on my nerves, and I cringed at the idea of them having Mixed children to show off as trophies or taint with their confusion.

As far as I could tell, my mother fell into the former category and my father fell into the latter. Maybe that's part of what drew them together or what drove them apart. All I knew was that sex and romance weren't necessarily as "color blind" as some people liked to believe. And love did not always override racism to conquer all.

Chapter 30: Greener

After I completed my second year at the University of Washington, it was more evident than ever that a communications degree from that school wouldn't include the hands-on film and television experience I needed to reach my goals. Greg's Big Brother, Ed Samuelsson, told me about a quirky place called The Evergreen State College, which he swore was the perfect place for a self-directed, non-conformist learner like me. Following Ed's advice, I applied, and was delighted to be accepted.

Evergreen was a fairly new alternative school situated in the woods of Olympia, Washington's state capital. Instead of offering the traditional grades, tests and pre-fab curricula of the University of Washington and other mainstream schools, Evergreen encouraged students to design their own educational experience. Best of all, it offered a new hands-on film and television studies program where I could develop skills and gain experience. We learned to operate cameras, lights and sound equipment. We also learned to edit. Classes were built around watching and analyzing different genres of movies, and we were encouraged to express our opinions without being pressured to conform for a grade. It was exhilarating!

The Evergreen thrills continued when I met Evergreen professor Joye Hardiman, an enchanting, elegant Black dynamo with proud features, natural hair and the most confident stride I'd ever seen. Joye was like a personal trainer for my brain. She pushed my intellect and stretched my creativity in never-ending discussions about the state of artistic aesthetics and expressions, race, and the Black community. A native New Yorker, she was adjusting to the presence of so many racially Mixed people in the Pacific Northwest. We talked a lot about my identity, and she had me read the works of Joel Augustus

Rogers, a Jamaican-American man who wrote about ethnic Africans, including those who were Mixed, to show the connections between people in different countries.

Joye—who resembled the stunning musical artist and activist Nina Simone—shared my passion for dissecting and addressing colorism. When I wondered how my appearance would fit into the movement for change, she assigned me to re-read one of my favorite books. The Spook Who Sat by the Door by Sam Greenlee was the story of Dan Freeman, a Black man who became a CIA agent, then took his knowledge to gangs in the ghetto and organized them to overthrow the racist system that oppressed them. I'd also seen the great movie version of the book, which was pulled from theatres after just a few days for fear that it would incite a real-life revolution.

In the book, when Pretty Willie, a light-skinned Mixed gang member, seemed unsure about his place in the struggle, Dan Freeman coached him and the other light-skinned guys to disguise themselves as White guys to rob banks for the revolution's war chest. After the robberies, they changed from their suits and ties to regular clothes, laughing while the police sought White bank robbers, never dreaming that Black guys had pulled off a major heist.

With Pretty Willie, Sam Greenlee illustrated that everybody had a role to play in the struggle, while demonstrating how the currency of light skin and ambiguous appearance could be used for the greater good.

Joye's mentor, Dr. at Evergreen, Dr. Maxine Mimms, was a fiercely brilliant and beautiful warrior woman who had created "The Tacoma Group," a program designed to help working-class Black people south of Seattle build upon their life and professional experience to earn a college degree. Maxine grew the program into an acclaimed satellite school focused on community empowerment. Her classes on The Nature of Community were rousing, challenging seminars that connected students' perspectives to the issues of the day. Without pretense or fanfare. Maxine skillfully guided students to share their life stories, and then to consider those stories in a broader context of connectivity. Her classes were followed by impromptu discussions over scrumptious feasts at The Caballeros, a nearby soul food restaurant.

I was nervous when Maxine assigned me to stand in front of the class and talk about being Mixed. I wasn't sure how this roomful of elders who had survived Jim Crow and the aftermath would feel about my ideas. Unlike the group of mental health professionals I'd shared my story with a decade earlier, these were my classmates, not strangers. They were Black, not White. I knew most of their stories but had no idea how they would receive mine. I was sharing deeply personal parts of myself that might reflect or conflict with theirs.

To calm my nerves and focus my energy, I closed my eyes and recalled Mom's voice saying, "You have to be able to look in the mirror and face your own truth." I pictured the little Mixed kids I was seeing everywhere and remembered how much I wished for someone to help them navigate this color-obsessed world. Inspired, I opened up to share the twists and turns that had forged my sense of self. I confided my soul-deep yearning for a word that didn't require amputating parts of my ancestry. Some of my classmates looked intrigued, others perplexed and a few downright resistant.

One woman asked if I'd ever passed for White. "Not deliberately," I answered, "except when dealing with the police. Some people think I'm White, but I don't know ahead of time what anyone thinks I am." A man with greying hair said that he had Mixed grandchildren. "Do you ever wish you weren't Mixed?" he asked. I shook my head. "No. But, to be honest, there are times when I've wished my appearance made my identity instantly obvious at first glance."

Then some of them shared what they thought I was before the presentation: Greek. Italian. Native American. Chicana. Samoan. Creole. And one woman said, "Well before today I wasn't exactly sure, but I knew you were sumthin.'"

The 1980 Census

Unlike on the previous census counts, the wording "Color or Race" was not used in 1980. This time, the race question included response categories for four racial groups: White, Black, American Indian or Alaskan Native, and Asian or Pacific Islanders.

This was the first census to identify Hispanics as an ethnic group that could be of any race, and to collect data on Hispanics rather than automatically classifying them as White.

The American Indian category widened to include Canadian Indians, French-American Indians and Spanish-American Indians. The Asian/Pacific Islander category included people who identified as Chinese, Filipino, Japanese, Asian Indian, Korean, Vietnamese, Hawaiian, Samoan, Guamanian, Cambodian, Laotian, Pakistani or Fiji Islander. Write-ins of Nipponese and Japanese American were counted as Japanese, and Taiwanese and Cantonese as Chinese.

In a departure from 1970, when they were counted as White, people who wrote in Cuban, Puerto Rican, Mexican or Dominican were counted as

"Other race."

If a person listed multiple races, the race of his or her mother was used. In another change from the 1970 census, the terms "Brown," "Mulatto" and other designations could be entered under "Other."

TaRessa at 23

Chapter 31: The Seattle Conundrum

The Evergreen State College was all about experiential learning. I was interested in becoming an independent filmmaker. When I got the opportunity to promote a big-deal Black film festival that came through Seattle, Joye assigned me to interview the group of independent filmmakers to better inform my own career goals.

Absorbing the wisdom of the brilliantly talented Haile Gerima, Reginald Hudlin and his brother Warrington Hudlin, Carol Monday Lawrence, Charles Burnett and festival organizer Oliver Franklin regarding their creative hustles and struggles changed my life. Hearing about the ups and downs of the independent filmmaking life, I realized that I wasn't cut out for the years of seeking financing and challenges of finding distribution for the film itself. I didn't have a clear vision for the kind of films I wanted to make, but I wasn't attracted to the idea of the mainstream Hollywood route. These revelations forced me to find new career goals.

Since I loved to write and had a knack for marketing, I switched my focus to publicity and public relations. After graduation, I was in demand and able to get a good job with the local PBS station.

Joye remained my mentor, and together we worked with many talented local artists whose work was grounded in expressing the richness of Black culture. Through theatre, poetry, visual arts, music, dance, film and video we moved through the early 1980s creating work that was affirmative, inspiring and hopefully empowering.

Still, I had to grapple both creatively and personally with Seattle's racial conundrums. My hometown was a great place to grow up Mixed. Its multicultural population and flavor provided a counterbalance to the city's overwhelming Whiteness, and the common presence of interracial couples and families allowed me to see myself as normal instead of an oddity. That gave me the confidence to feel true to myself on my identity journey.

But on the flip side, Seattle was named the fifth Whitest city in the country in 1980. It had Asians at 14%, Blacks at 7%, Hispanic/Latinos at 6,6%, Mixed people at 5.6%, and Native Americans at 0.4%.

Once I stepped outside of the creative cocoon of that small Black creative community, frustration set in. And too often when someone suggested something for the Black community, the immediate response was: "But we have to include others and make it multicultural."

Ironically, all of the other groups in "multicultural" also had their own institutions, programs, cultural centers and other resources. It seemed like Black people were the main ones being asked to prioritize multiculturalism over ethnocentric specificity. I was a huge fan of diverse alliances, but Joye taught me that you had to be fully grounded in your own identity and culture before you could successfully collaborate and join forces with others.

In the early 1980s for a Black single woman in Seattle, the biggest downside was the dating scene which was defined by angst over lots of Black men preferring any kind of woman to a Black woman. The saying was that most Black men would step over a Black woman to get to a White (or Asian) one. This wasn't all Black men, of course, but it was enough to earn Seattle a national reputation as a place where heterosexual Black women could choose between being dateless and frustrated or crossing the color lines to find romance. The nonstop conversations on the topic were even chronicled in the local newspapers. When my Black girlfriends and I saw an attractive Black guy, or a friend told us about someone they wanted us to meet, the first question was always: "Is he into White women?" It felt like an obsession. Yes, everyone was free to love who they wanted, but the prevalence made it feel like much more than a simple personal preference. The very dynamic that led to my conception was now working against me in my twenties.

One of my closest friends and running buddies was Sherry, a drop-dead gorgeous woman who was as dark as I was light. We went to parties and nightclubs with our hopes up, only to have them destroyed by men proving the Seattle stereotype by literally passing both of us by, or ignoring her to focus on me. While I wanted to be considered attractive, the pattern was too consistent for me to feel flattered. I was angry about the blatant colorism and wondered

Calvin II and Mariah, ages 5 and 3

TaRessa Stovall

what, if anything, I could do about it. Sherry never complained, but we were both frustrated by the fact that so few eligible Black men seemed to regard us as potential partners.

The irony of all this weighed on me. I flashed back to the refrain of my childhood: "White girls are better than you because…" and considered that my own father had never chosen a Black woman for a romantic partner. I recognized that I was the sum of that very equation. Though I was light-skinned and so-called "exotic" looking, some of those Black men who found me attractive quickly lost interest when they realized that my behavior conflicted with their need to fetishize my ambiguous appearance.

Thanks to White racism demanding so much of my time, energy and attention, I reasoned that being Black in America—in any percentage—equated to a full-time job. Unlike Whiteness, which was based on exclusivity and notions of purity, Black was inclusive, making room for my mother and other non-Black people who were welcomed into the community. Beyond the few Jewish things that Mom shared now and then, I wasn't familiar enough with Jewish culture for it to impact my sense of self. While it didn't have the zing of a single word or catchphrase, I was comfortable describing myself as Black with a Jewish mother.

Embracing that inclusive version of Blackness felt like reclaiming wholeness on my own terms, without having to compromise or meet anyone else's qualifications. The world could meet me where I lived, at the nexus of my messy and inconvenient complexity, or choose to do otherwise. I was learning that the only decisions and actions I could control were my own.

Chapter 32: Mecca

I was itching to get out of Seattle with no clear destination in mind. But the Universe came through in the form of Dr. Rosetta Hunter, a gorgeous college professor and longtime mentor to young people in the community. Rosie B, as we called her, had just returned from visiting her lovely daughter, Theresa, nicknamed Tee, in Atlanta. When Sherry and I greeted Rosie B and asked how Tee was doing, she smiled, "She's great. She loves it there." Before we could respond, Rosie B dropped her smile and fixed me with a piercing look. "You belong in Atlanta," she said.

I paused, breathless, with that ping in the gut that signified a message straight from the divine. Rosie B didn't have to tell me twice. I'd never really been to the South, but Atlanta's reputation was well known. For years, nearly every issue of every Black magazine extolled the virtues of the Black Mecca. Ever since Maynard Jackson became Atlanta's first Black mayor in 1973 at just thirty-five years old and expanded economic opportunities for people of color, Atlanta was known as a magnet for the young, gifted, Black and ambitious.

Sherry and I booked airline tickets and a reasonably priced downtown hotel for a ten-day visit in August 1985. A week before our departure date, we realized that neither of us knew a soul in Atlanta. Not wanting to wander the streets in desperation, I contacted some well-connected journalism friends, who shared the name of an Atlanta-based newspaper reporter and author, Roger Witherspoon.

I called Roger, who was writing a book about Dr. Martin Luther King, Jr., and he worked miracles. On the basis of a few well-placed questions about the kinds of jobs, social lives and men that Sherry and I were seeking, Roger created an itinerary worthy of visiting dignitaries. Our brilliant Atlanta guardian angel arranged meetings with people who hosted parties to welcome us, job networking opportunities and introductions to handsome single men. And he did it all before the internet, email, cell phones, texting, social media or GPS devices.

Atlanta opened her arms and we enthusiastically returned the embrace. Sherry and I didn't stop smiling for the whole ten days. With a sharp, good-looking Black mayor—charismatic former U.N. Ambassador Andrew Young—and other young, dynamic Black political leaders, impressive career opportunities and men galore, we had no doubt that Atlanta was the place for us.

When I told Mom I was moving to the South, she looked at me like I'd lost my mind. I realized her only association with that part of the country was the horrors of Jim Crow that caused millions of Black people to flee a generation before. I think she secretly prayed that I'd change my mind, but nothing would deter me. I called and wrote every Atlanta contact I made on my first visit, determined to secure gainful employment and escape Seattle at the earliest opportunity.

Soon, Sherry and I found jobs and settled in. I put my creative experience to work as executive director of The Neighborhood Arts Center, Atlanta's first Black arts center. After a fire at its previous location, the Center had relocated to the Odd Fellows building on historic "Sweet Auburn" Avenue, which had a rich and bittersweet history.

From the late 1800s through the mid 1900s, Auburn Avenue was nationally renowned as the South's most concentrated hub of Black commerce, entertainment, and spiritual uplift. In 1956, Fortune magazine called Auburn Avenue "the richest Negro street in the world." It was a thriving center of history, culture, and achievement where Black people, forced there by segregation, lived, worked, and conducted business with their own. Popular landmarks included the Royal Peacock upscale entertainment club, Big Bethel AME Church, First Congregational Church, the headquarters of the nation's first Black-owned daily newspaper, The Atlanta Daily World, and the Atlanta Life Insurance building--headquarters to the second-largest Black insurance company in the United States. Auburn Avenue is also rich with the history of civil rights, from Dr. Martin Luther King, Jr.,'s birth home, the King family church home, Ebenezer Baptist Church, and The Martin Luther King, Jr. Center for Nonviolent Social Change.

The decline of Auburn Avenue was an ironic side effect of the fight for equality. As the Civil Rights Movement, headed in part by Dr. King, the NAACP, and local voting rights groups worked from their offices in the area, the victory over the restrictions of segregation sent many business owners to other parts of the city. Though Auburn Avenue was designated a National Historic Landmark in 1976, when I went to work there a decade later, it had been split by a highway and devastated by crime, shuttered businesses and abandoned buildings.

The Neighborhood Arts Center, formed in 1975, became part of Auburn Avenue shortly before I arrived. The Center, known as NAC, was created as a model for community arts in areas of Atlanta that had not traditionally been exposed to culture. Its history included such talents as visual artist Romare Bearden, actors Samuel L. Jackson and Bill Nunn, author Toni Cade Bambara, and countless others working in varying creative disciplines.

The Neighborhood Arts Center turned a former storefront on the ground floor into an art gallery, with our offices and space for artists' studios upstairs. I felt deeply honored and humbled to be working with this iconic institution in the historic building on the legendary street. As I walked the length of Auburn Avenue, I felt its spirits whispering to my soul.

Dr. Otis T. Hammonds, the founder, guiding light and financial benefactor of NAC, was a renowned medical doctor and anesthesiologist who was also an avid art collector, staunch local arts patron, gardener, and community leader. He served as chairman of the NAC board of directors until he passed away in 1985. The members of the board of directors were a super-smart, multi-talented group who cared deeply about continuing the center's proud legacy. They were generous with their time and guidance in helping me in my new position, and patient as I learned to soften my brash, straightforward communication style to work the softer, less direct Atlanta way.

Atlanta, then nicknamed "Hotlanta," was known for its large population of well-educated, ambitious idealistic Black people--largely Baby Boomers—who were infused with a sense that they could realize their dreams among like-minded people. The city pulsed with rich Black history, culture and pride. While nobody denied or downplayed the existence of racism, it was faced as a fact of life and not a deterrent to achieving one's goals. This intoxicating rush of energy and possibility nurtured my famished soul.

Best of all, Atlanta was full of single Black men our age who didn't seem infected with the "anything but a Black woman" fever that plagued my hometown. I even found guys who were attracted to me—not my light skin or my hair and not because they thought I was "exotic" or a two-fer.

TaRessa Stovall

For the first time, I wasn't asked to pass the "What are you?" test. I was just another light-skinned "redbone," and I didn't stand out at all. Interracial couples were so rare as to be practically nonexistent, and nobody talked about Black men rejecting Black women.

Southern-fried anti-Black racism from White people was refreshingly straightforward, aboveboard and matter-of-fact. Unlike liberal, progressive Seattle, where letting your guard down meant you could be blindsided by racist gaslighting, the Atlanta version of racial bias left no room for surprise or confusion. Because the White people didn't feel guilty or ashamed of their racism, they didn't try to sugarcoat it or pretend to be apologetic. I found this version much less stressful than the kind back home.

As in any environment where People of Color are in the majority, it was easy to see the light-skinned-dark-skinned dynamic at work. Colorism--the term popularized by literary supernova Alice Walker to describe both interracial and intraracial prejudice based on skin tone and preference for light skin--was an integral part of African American history from day one. It had wound its way through enslavement, emancipation, Reconstruction, Jim Crow and the Civil Rights and Black Power movements. This insidious form of discrimination was always ready to rear its head. As Atlanta author and playwright Pearl Cleage wrote in her popular play, Flyin' West, "you ever seen a group of colored people that didn't put the lightest one in charge?"

An early reminder of how colorism impacted our everyday expectations and interactions came in my first weeks working with the Neighborhood Arts Center. I was struggling to set up a visual arts display for an arts fair in Piedmont Park. While several people had signed up to help, only one man showed up. He was a forty-ish stranger, quiet and hard-working, with deep brown skin, a salt-and-pepper beard and a tentative smile. His eight-year-old son was with him. We worked in the relentless heat and humidity to get the exhibit together. His son pitched in, too. I brought us some cool lemonade throughout the day. The first time, the son accepted his with a quick, "Thank you, ma'am," but the father hesitated, asking "How much do I owe you?"

"Nothing," I said. "I couldn't have done any of this without you. I am so grateful for your help."

A man of few words, he accepted the lemonade with a quick nod. Hours later, as we were tearing down the exhibit, he spoke up. "I have to admit something," he said. "You don't act the way you look. You know, the way that I expected you to be. You're nice to me. You get what I'm saying?"

I nodded woodenly, caught between understanding and shame. "I get

Greg and me featured in the article, Seattle's Interracial Children: A Question of Choice and Pride, about campaigning for a Mixed-race census category, in the September 7, 1978, issue of Jet magazine

it," I said, thanking him and his son again for their help. As they walked away, I lingered in the setting sun, digesting the significance of his words. Part of me wanted to be irate: Why'd he have to stereotype me like that? But I knew he'd had a lifetime of painful reasons to expect me to treat him and his son "a certain way." The truth of his experience wasn't debatable.

The fleeting pleasure of being told that I was an exception was eclipsed by sorrow at the overwhelming presence of the rule. I considered myself committed to the cause, and hyper-vigilant about colorism when I encountered it. But that wasn't enough to keep me from failing my best friend, Sherry.

Unlike the situation in Seattle, Sherry got plenty of positive attention from men in Atlanta, where her beauty was much more valued and appreciated.

A prominent businessman friend of ours hosted a party. As Sherry and I walked in, I was checking out the men. Our host greeted me with a big smile and a warm hug, and I stepped into the room of good-looking possibilities. Sherry came in behind me. As I turned to ask where she wanted to sit, I saw the hurt on her face. "You didn't stick up for me!" she said in a low, angry voice.

I was perplexed. "What happened?" I asked, looking around. "Did somebody--"

"Didn't you see how he just ignored me after he gave you that great big hug?" she asked, gesturing towards our host friend.

"I really didn't notice," I mumbled. "I'm so sorry, I didn't see."

"That's the problem." Sherry said dejectedly.

I felt horrible. She was right. We both knew the dynamic too well. While we'd escaped the Seattle issues, colorism was everywhere. I forgot about eyeballing the men in the room and parked in front of the food table, stress-eating crudités while wondering what I could say or do. Was it my place to call him--a dark-skinned person--out for how he treated another dark-skinned person? And even if I had the words, would it really change their behavior? The guilt, shame, and frustration of not being able to solve the equation stayed with me for a long time.

Just as Sheryl and I did back in my childhood, Sherry and I avoided the topic after that incident. But I couldn't stop wondering about what I could have done. Who was I to even think about taking on the hydra-headed monster of color-struck culture? It was too widespread, too deeply embedded and much too pervasive to wrap my brain around solutions. And though I tried to stay aware of its ever-present threat, there was always the risk that I'd fail to notice when it was about to strike someone I loved.

TaRessa Stovall

Chapter 33: Spelman

When I moved to Atlanta in the mid-1980s, the city boasted about its diversity. Being from Seattle, I scoffed at this claim. Then I realized that in this growing metropolis, diversity meant that Black people and White people were increasingly comfortable occupying the same spaces.

While folks weren't asking about my racial category, I did bump into assumptions about my education and, by extension, my class background. Many people's first words to me were, "You're a Spelman woman, right?" I didn't know much about the prestigious Black women's college, but quickly learned of its reputation for excellence and the stereotype that most of its students and alumnae were "high-class," which often translated to light-skinned.

One of my first and favorite Atlanta contacts was a wonderful woman named Jo Moore Stewart, who ran Spelman's communications department. Seduced by the positive energy of the tiny campus, I told Jo that I wanted to work there. Months later, she informed me that Spelman was looking for a director of public relations and encouraged me to apply.

The Neighborhood Arts Center was recovering from the loss of Dr. Hammond, and I was overwhelmed by the responsibilities of running a non-profit, especially the nonstop demands of fundraising. After a series of interviews for the job at Spelman, I was smitten with the small, magical campus. I shared my hopes of getting the job with my boyfriend, a regal dark-skinned man with sculpted cheekbones and down-home Southern smarts. "Do you think I'll get it?" I asked anxiously.

He shot me a look that said it all.

I hated the thought that I might be hired because of what I looked like. "But what about my fabulous resume?" I wondered, realizing that I had to reevaluate all of the professional praise I'd ever received, all of the opportunities I'd thought I earned and deserved.

Though it was uncomfortable to fully acknowledge that I'd long benefited from preferential treatment, I couldn't ignore the role it played not only in my career, but in every option and opportunity throughout my life. For so long, I'd been told how smart, talented, creative and capable I was. But what if the only reason I'd ever gotten the job, or the guy, or the access to anything was because of the way I did—and more importantly, did not—look?

I twisted and turned through a week of sleepless nights until I learned that I'd gotten the job as director of public relations at Spelman College. Despite my misgivings about the colorism aspect, I secretly hoped they'd hired me at least in part because they thought I was right for the job. My colleagues represented the full spectrum of color, and while they were warm and welcoming, they didn't seem at all concerned or impressed with my appearance. Colorism was not evident in our day-to-day interactions.

I started in January 1987, when students were on holiday break. Jo and my boss helped to immerse me in Spelman history and culture as the college narrowed its search for president—its very first Black woman president—to four candidates. It was an exciting time.

One Thursday morning after the students returned to campus from their winter break, Jo invited me to attend Convocation—the weekly gathering of students in the beautifully quaint Sisters Chapel to hear inspiring words from a campus luminary or Black leader. Based on the long-standing stereotypes about Spelman, I worried that I'd see a building full of very light-skinned, straight-haired girls. I held my breath and entered the chapel. It was a relief to see that the students clad in traditional white dresses and pearls represented the full rainbow of Black beauty. Light-skinned students weren't even close to the majority. The energy of these young women and the sense of sisterhood were absolutely delicious.

When Dr. Johnnetta B. Cole was selected as the first Sister President, I was elated. Along with her stunning presence and elegant charm, she brought a kind of brilliance I hadn't experienced since Joye Hardiman back at Evergreen. Sitting with Dr. Cole, you could literally see her mind working like the highest-quality precision machine—sharing words, ideas and philosophies that were as accessible as they were inspiring and profound.

Tall and light-skinned with bluish-green eyes, Dr. Cole wore a short, sculpted Afro and proudly displayed her collection of African art in the president's house. She wove Afrocentric touches into her wardrobe and that influence spread throughout the campus. Soon more students were sporting natural hair and African-inspired outfits, headwraps and jewelry. The campus was electrified by her warm, generous spirit and open-hearted style of "presidenting," as she called it.

Dr. Cole was so popular with the media that I worked overtime managing the requests for interviews and appearances. Together, we worked to maximize Spelman's stellar reputation as a powerhouse dedicated to producing women who were global thinkers and servant-leaders.

At Spelman, I learned to bask in the complexity of Black womanhood and appreciate how the students' race and gender were centralized, normalized, nurtured, and affirmed. I was honored to be part of this unique community, which was so much richer, deeper, and more beautifully diverse than many people realized. Not only did the students, faculty, staff and alumnae represent every class background and geographic area around the U.S .and the world, but they projected a confidence in their own brains and talent that was contagious. While I didn't attend Spelman, I considered the four years that I served the college as director of public relations essential to the development of my identity.

Spelman and Atlanta helped me to understand and appreciate the multi-dimensional diversity of Black people from throughout the Diaspora. Blackness had never felt so expansive, so multi-faceted, or so free.

The 1990 Census

The main difference between the 1980 and 1990 census forms is that "race" was put back into the wording. Three categories required write-ins: Indian (Amer.) to specify the name of their tribe; and those who reported "Other Asian or Pacific Islander" or "Other race" wrote in the name of their group or race. The Census Bureau tested a version that didn't include a separate listing of detailed Asian and Pacific Islander groups, but members of that community protested for the more specific listing.

Chapter 34: Vision of Love

In the summer of 1989, I was 30-something, enjoying my job at Spelman and casually dating a couple of guys. To upgrade my long-term prospects, I was seeing a therapist to do the inner work for attracting a healthy, lasting relationship. For fun, I followed the advice of some happily married Spelman coworkers and wrote a list of everything I wanted in a man. Then I tucked the list away and basically forgot about it.

Though I was working on my daddy issues, I wasn't prepared for my father to reach out.

He'd moved from Seattle to Wisconsin a couple years earlier. Then, as I was paying a professional $75 an hour to help me make sense of our contentious bond, he called me out of the blue and asked me to send him a picture and letter about how my life was going. I'd spent so much time being either angry or disappointed with him that I didn't know how to respond.

Mom helped me process this baffling request. She explained that he was in his seventies with lots of health problems and that I needed to reconcile with him if I wanted better relationship outcomes for myself. I was skeptical but did as he asked. He shocked me even more by inviting me to visit him.

I froze, terrified at the idea. We were near-strangers with an adversarial history. What could he want from me? Mom repeated her advice, warning that I didn't want to be weighed down with regret if he passed away before we'd made some kind of peace.

My anxiety was so overwhelming that I could barely board the plane. Dad's longtime wife picked me up at the airport, explaining that he was too sick to leave their small home. I barely recognized Dad, sitting quietly in a recliner. He was as sharply dressed as ever, with his Stacy Adams shoes shined to a high gloss. He took handfuls of medications for various ailments and could barely talk. We hugged awkwardly and spoke haltingly. He didn't have an appetite, but asked me to make a fruit salad and did his best to eat it with a smile.

He asked his wife to play music by jazz saxophonist Dexter Gordon, which took me back to two poignant scenes.

Years earlier, when I was in my mid-twenties we both still lived in Seattle, Dad shocked me with an invitation to accompany him to hear Dexter Gordon at a local jazz club. I nervously accepted, hoping that maybe we could actually get to know something about each other.

The six-foot-five Dexter Gordon, nicknamed "Long Tall Dex," played beautifully. Mostly, my eyes were on my father's face, watching the interplay of emotions as he listened to the music, wondering what memories and sensations it stirred. But I had no idea how to ask or even begin a conversation with him. As long as the music played, we were spared from having to talk. During the breaks, we both fidgeted and avoided each other's eyes. He didn't say much beyond banal small talk, and he sounded shy, uncertain of his words. I replied, but couldn't find the rhythm to maintain a dialogue.

When I told Mom about it, she explained that Dad was much quieter and reserved when he was sober. Since he'd been a disciplined weekend alcoholic during my childhood and that was the only time I'd seen him, this man at the Dexter Gordon concert was a stranger to me.

Now, sitting with my father, listening to his Dexter Gordon album in his small Wisconsin home, brought back memories of the second poignant scene. I recalled seeing the film "'Round Midnight," which rocked my world with its eerie parallels to the tensions between Dad and me. In that film, Dexter Gordon portrayed a drug-addicted musician who left the USA for Paris to get his life together. On a visit back to the States, the musician reached out to his Mixed-race teenage daughter, trying to connect with her. When she came to see him play in a nightclub on her birthday, he proudly introduced her to the audience, but got her age wrong. Later, they met in a diner, the energy between them as awkward and stilted as mine had been with my father. When the musician character mumbled an apology to his daughter for not bringing her any gifts from Paris, she said sadly, "I didn't expect anything."

"I didn't expect anything." Those four words summed up my entire relationship with my father. That scene replayed in my mind as I sat in his Wisconsin living room. Though we didn't speak much, the energy in the room was warm and forgiving. In a strange, wordless way, Dad and I apologized to each other. The rage that had sustained me throughout my childhood melted into waves of sadness at all the father-daughter moments we'd never get to share. I still didn't know enough about his life. I had no idea whether he liked me or was proud of me or had ever read a single thing I'd written. We'd never know each other's hopes, dreams, fears, or wishes. The gulf that separated us required more than two days of halting words and regretful glances. But it was a start. We parted with warm hugs, and I headed home.

I wasn't looking for love or particularly interested in marriage. But a few months after my visit with Dad, I met the love of my life, at a journalists' convention in New York City. A mutual friend introduced me to Calvin Stovall, a sharply dressed newspaper editor with caramel skin, twinkling green eyes and a sweet grin. As we hung out, I learned that this soft-spoken Southern boy was whip-smart with a charmingly sarcastic wit that made me laugh.

Calvin swept me off my feet in a whirlwind romance. I was thrilled to note that he had most of the qualities on the list I'd written describing my ideal man. Within months, we fell deeply in love, became engaged, and bought a home in Atlanta. We married in our backyard with cherished family and friends in attendance. Weeks later, we conceived our first child.

Halfway through the pregnancy, Calvin was offered a prestigious position in the Washington, D.C. area, so we left Atlanta to head "Up South" to the nation's capital. In the midst of this, my father passed away. I deeply regretted missed opportunities and words unsaid between us, but there were no tears because I'd been grieving him for most of my life. I was glad I'd followed Mom's advice and tried to connect with the man so I could move beyond the empty spaces he'd left in my heart and soul.

Thrilled to be expecting and too obviously pregnant to look for a job, I took long walks to explore my new Washington, D.C. habitat, and frequent naps to grow the bouncing baby boy I carried with trepidation and pride. It was 1991, and the videotaped police beating of Rodney King by Los Angeles police played on endless television news loops. I channeled my horror and anxieties into my first newspaper column, which was about growing a Black manchild in the belly of the beast that was America's racial strife. .

Calvin II was born at nearly 10 pounds that summer, a blonde, blue-eyed bundle of high energy and joy. Our son's skin was the color of mine. His blue eyes could have come from either my mother or his father. The blond hair was from my husband's solidly African-American side of the family—there wasn't a natural blond strand anywhere on my side of the family tree.

Immersed in new motherhood and still adjusting to being a newlywed, I worked on my first book. It attracted the interest of a leading New York City literary agent. She coached me through a few rewrites, and then reached out to help me find a publisher. I got some interest and a lot of positive feedback, but no solid offers.

I shelved the book and got a job. Our daughter, Mariah, was born in late summer, two years and one month younger than her big brother. She was light brown with dark hair and eyes. Despite the differences in their coloring and sizes, Calvin II and Mariah's features were so similar that strangers often asked if they were twins. I felt bad that I'd doomed my children to being racially ambiguous-looking, but relieved that I could at least understand enough about what they would go through to be able to discuss the issues openly and help them navigate the challenges I knew were ahead. I also felt confident that I could talk frankly with them about the politics of skin color and hair dynamics, both in the Black community and beyond.

With an infant and a toddler, life moved quickly. There was no room or need to think about my Mixed identity. I was firmly part of a Black family (with a Jewish Baubie) and that was that. We filled our modest suburban home with Black and diverse books, toys, and art.

I was consumed with wanting to be a great wife and mother. The mother part was easy, since mine was such a great role model. The wife part was more challenging, because I'd never seen a warm, happy, loving marriage close-up. I over-compensated for my daddy issues by focusing on pleasing Calvin and making sure that he was happy. I didn't just put myself on the back burner—I pushed myself off of the stove completely. I reasoned that if my family was healthy and happy, the rest would figure itself out.

I squeezed in moments of writing when I could. At 40, I was more determined than ever to build a successful career as an author. I was passionate about filling the void in examples of strong, positive Black love stories and marriages. My literary agent liked the idea, and Calvin agreed to lend his journalistic expertise to the project. Soon, we had a deal from Time Warner for A Love Supreme: Real-Life Stories of Black Love.

We traveled together to interview couples. A few were well-known, but we wanted to focus on the love stories of people from different generations and backgrounds who lived their lives outside of the spotlight. A Love Supreme... was published in February 2000. Since it was both Black History Month and the season for Valentine's Day, the book attracted a fair amount of media coverage—including a brief spot on the "In the Spirit" segment of The Oprah

Winfrey Show. That was back in the days when publishers invested in book tours, and we traveled to a handful of carefully selected cities to enthusiastic receptions.

Ironically, our own marriage was on shaky ground. It was like a hurricane of emotional chaos, tearing us apart. There was never any question that we loved each other, but with the perspective that comes with time and working through a long grieving process, I understand that we simply didn't have the tools to navigate some of the challenges that rocked our world. It's easy to crave comforting, easy answers in an emotional post-mortem. But the truth was that Calvin and I weren't equipped as a couple to survive the storm. We reached out to several people for help, but none were able to provide the guidance that might have kept us together.

Even as our hearts were breaking while our decade-long marriage crumbled, we fought hard to keep the children first and foremost. It took a great deal of work, but we were able to build a respectful, amicable co-parenting relationship focused on the kids' well-being. In some ways, the skills we developed during that process might have served us well as a couple. But I'm satisfied that our children had close, nurturing relationships with both us and never questioned or doubted that we loved them and put their well-being above all else.

Ironically, in the midst of the turmoil and tumult of the year 2000—when A Love Supreme was published and my marriage was on life support—the United States Census made a longtime dream of mine come true. Kind of.

Chapter 35: "Some Other Race"

The 2000 Census was the first to include an option for people to identify as more than one race. The question "What is this person's race?" allowed the option to "Mark one or more races to indicate what this person considers himself/herself to be." At the bottom, after all of the specific categories, was a box and the words, "Some other race – Print race."

I wanted to be impressed with this new category. But the phrasing of "some other race" felt like a throwaway, too vague to convey respect or be taken seriously. And what would the Census Bureau do with the numbers it collected from that section?

By then, I knew that census data was used to determine critical resources including legislative districts, school district assignment areas, and seats in the U.S. House of Representatives. The ways that census data were compiled impacted where roads were built and services were provided for the elderly, as well as how billions of dollars in federal funds were allocated to local, state, and tribal governments for neighborhood improvements, public health, education, transportation, and more.

It wasn't clear how the folks who did check more than one box or fill in the "Some Other Race" field would be tallied. Would they be counted as off-handedly as they'd been asked to identify themselves? I reasoned that the decision was political, not personal, for me. The way I filled out the form could affect many people and their quality of life. I couldn't justify making a mark for Mixed presence and pride if there was a chance it would work against the Black community.

While I'd wanted to feel more excited about this "new" category, it looked like a government set-up for Mixed people to choose between personal expression and awareness of how the census data was used to shape communities and determine resources. So, I checked "Black, African Am, or Negro," because it included the entire spectrum of African-American history and culture. It embraced the rainbow of skin tones, the countless hair textures. It included space for those of us with a parent who wasn't Black as well.

Beyond the issue of categories, I continued obsessing about colorism, though I still didn't have any concrete solutions. In 1992, when I was pregnant with Mariah, a homegirl invited me to take part in an independent documentary film titled "Black Women On: The Light/Dark Thang." The film was made by two television veterans and friends—Paula Caffey, who was light-skinned, and Celeste Crenshaw, who was dark-skinned. It presented a wonderful opportunity for women of all shades to commune and share our stories and feelings about the topic that impacted all of us deeply.

"Black Women On: The Light/Dark Thang" was shown widely on PBS stations around the country in the late 1990s, winning an Emmy Award for Celeste and Paula. The glow from that experience fed my hunger to find ways to address this issue and spark some change.

Speaking of change, life had more in store. In 1998, Calvin got an exciting new job that relocated us to Southern New Jersey. We moved to Mount Laurel, a moderately diverse town that was more working-class than our Northern Virginia suburb had been. I took on more consulting clients, which enabled me to work from home and focus on our children. We were still working to finish the "Love Supreme" book and consider how to best address the needs of our aging parents who lived in different states.

That move must have exposed deep fault lines in our marriage, because Calvin and I faced new struggles as a couple. There was never any question that we loved each other deeply and were committed to our little family. But we couldn't overcome the unhealed wounds that each of us had brought to our union and that ultimately pushed us apart. After more than a year of struggling to patch our marriage together, my divorce from Calvin was final in the fall of 2001, just weeks after 9/11 devastated our New Jersey community and our sense of the world.

As I searched for a new home that allowed our kids to stay in their school, and started learning to live on a single income, my mother turned to me for help with her health challenges. She had surgery for a heart condition she'd inherited from her mother and later developed cancer. Fiercely independent, Mom ignored doctors' warnings that she should no longer live alone and stay in the Seattle home where we grew up. I begged her to move in with us, but she stalled, reluctant to leave her sanctuary of more than fifty years. I felt her anxiety and pain. All of her siblings had passed away, and many of her closest friends were gone or ailing. She worked into her eighties, as long as her health allowed and finally, in 2006, she reluctantly agreed to live with us.

The year before, the children and I had moved to the charmingly eclectic Northern New Jersey town of Montclair. It was more racially diverse and sophisticated than our Southern New Jersey suburb had been. I wanted Calvin II and Mariah to experience their teens in a progressive, walkable, child-centric small-town atmosphere while learning to navigate New York City a dozen miles away. I felt at home in this village of creative, literary, and media folks.

I got a job at the weekly community newspaper which gave me the flexibility to tend to Mom and the kids as needed. Two highlights of that job altered the course of my identity journey. One was interviewing Lisa Williamson Rosenberg, professional ballerina-turned-psychotherapist, who spoke about being Black and Jewish in a local synagogue. I was almost giddy talking to Lisa, whose background was similar to mine. While I wasn't ready to wave the flag for Mixed identity, it was delightful to meet someone with whom I had so much in common. And it made me a little sad that I hadn't met more folks like me throughout my life

The second highlight that impacted my identity journey was the chance to interview cosmetics mogul Bobbi Brown for the newspaper. At the end of my interview, Bobbi (who is Jewish), studied my face and asked, "What are you?"

"Guess," I said, expecting one of the usual assumptions.

Within seconds she said confidently, "Black and Jewish." I was shocked—people never got it right. "You know—Blewish," she grinned.

"Blewish," I laughed, liking the way it tasted. I liked the fact that it told so much of my story in two succinct syllables and that it represented the synthesis of my different ancestries rather than focusing on racial fractions. Most of all, I was stunned that someone had correctly identified my ancestry, my bloodlines, and my mix, at first glance. I was thrilled at the novel sensation and sad that it was so rare.

Chapter 36: Inkblot Test

While being Mixed-race has its challenges and being light-skinned has its advantages and complications, being racially ambiguous-looking adds an extra layer of complexity. In a world that runs on assumptions about identity and rushes to assign categories, I find that the ambiguous dynamic impacts—and often intrudes upon—my everyday adult life. It's important to note that not all Mixed people are racially ambiguous-looking, and not all racially ambiguous-looking people are Mixed. But my experiences at the intersection of the two continue to require my diligent attention.

The greatest thrill of my years at Seward Elementary School was my first teacher-crush in the third grade. Ms. Gonzales was a bit browner than me, younger than my previous teachers, very glamorous, and proud of her Mexican heritage. Her sweet voice had the soft tinge of a Spanish accent. Her hair was even similar to mine: it started out smooth in the morning and by the end of the day, the frizz broke free.

Best of all, her eyes lit up when she looked at me. When she greeted each student at the classroom door each morning with her wide bright smile, she welcomed me in Spanish, pronouncing my formal name with a Spanish flair. She taught me to respond in Spanish and rewarded me with a special wink and a pat on the shoulder for my efforts. I glowed with pride.

When her eyes scanned the classroom and landed on me, I felt the warmth of our special bond. Top grades had always come easily to me, but I worked extra hard to be her favorite student, volunteering at every opportunity and campaigning hard for the title of teacher's pet. I talked so much about the marvelous Ms. Gonzales at home that Mom finally asked if I wanted to invite her over for dinner. Since Mom's cooking was the way to everyone's heart, I quickly agreed. Wanting it to be a really special occasion, I asked Mom if we could do something different: a traditional Jewish Friday night Shabbat meal. We didn't normally celebrate Jewish holidays or eat the foods, but I wanted to highlight Mom's heritage like Ms. Gonzales sometimes shared hers in the classroom.

I was excited to invite Ms. Gonzales, and she happily accepted my invitation for dinner the following Friday night. Mom worked extra hard the night before to make sure that every dish was just right. She even let me help prepare the matzoh balls for the fresh chicken soup and noodle kugel to accompany the brisket.

Friday dawned, and I jumped out of bed, eager to begin what I knew would be a magical day. After morning recess at school, Ms. Gonzalez pulled me aside to confirm the time for dinner and our address. Unable to keep the best part to myself, I shared that we were having a very special Jewish Shabbat celebration in her honor.

I noticed the strange expression on her face, but it didn't register as cause for alarm. The rest of the school day, I fidgeted at my desk, imagining the delight of bringing my beloved teacher into my home to enjoy Mom's delicious cooking.

Mom picked us up early, and we made a trip to Brenner Brothers Bakery for fresh challah. We raced home and I eagerly set the table with our fanciest dishes and holiday silverware. About a half hour before Ms. Gonzalez was to arrive, the phone rang. Mom answered it, nodding slowly, her forehead puckering, her lips clamped tight. "That's fine. I understand. Thank you for letting me know," she said in a terse voice before signing off the call.

Shaking her head, she lit a cigarette, took a deep drag, and then set it in the beanbag ashtray. She called me over and wrapped me in her arms. "That was Ms. Gonzales," she said sadly. "She explained that she can't come to our Shabbat dinner because she didn't realize we were Jewish. She thought you were Mexican, like her. She apologized for the misunderstanding, and said she'll see you in school on Monday."

I understood each word my mother said, but I couldn't comprehend the totality of her message. My brain was unable to process the fact that Ms. Gonzales wasn't coming to this magnificent meal that we'd gone to so much trouble to prepare in her honor because we were the wrong thing. We sat awkwardly at the specially-set table and ate the fancy meal in silence. I forced myself to chew and swallow the delicious food, which tasted like sawdust.

I spent the weekend lying in bed in the fetal position, sobbing until I fell asleep, then waking to sob some more. My eight-year-old heart was shattered, and even Mom's tender hugs and gentle words of reassurance didn't help. I tormented myself wondering: had I failed Ms. Gonzales, or had she failed me? What could I have done differently?

I didn't want to go to school on Monday, but Mom made me. As I neared the classroom, my stomach was knotted with anxiety. Ms. Gonzales greeted each student at the door as usual. When she started to greet me—in English—I rushed to my seat, eyes on the ground. I ached inside, missing the warm greetings, special smiles and winks we used to exchange back when she thought I was the same as her.

That was the day I stopped loving school. I no longer cared about Ms. Gonzales or anything she said. Instead, I replayed life before and after her Friday night phone call. If only she'd asked, I kept thinking. If only she'd asked.

Days later, when I finally allowed myself to meet her eyes, I saw only dullness there. I fought tears, longing to know why I'd been special to her only when she mistook me for being Mexican. Why now she acted like I didn't even exist.

I wanted to tell Ms. Gonzales that if she had a problem with Jews, she needed to know that I was Black and Native American too. So, if she wanted to hate me for what I was, she could at least be accurate and hate all of me, not just half.

That heartbreak taught me the pitfalls of building a relationship with someone based on what they assumed me to be.

What Ms. Gonzales really taught me is how dangerous it was to trust my identity to the eye of the beholder. Since then, I have learned that there are three kinds of identity beholders.

There are the beholders who hope—the people who rush up to me to breathlessly ask whether I am one of them. I can tell these beholders by the spark in their eyes as they approach, by the quiver of excitement and anticipation in their voices as they inquire: Are you (Greek, Italian, Israeli, Egyptian, Mexican/Chicana, Samoan, Puerto Rican, Cuban, Samoan, Creole, Trinidadian, Portuguese, Brazilian, Spanish, Filipina, Chinese)? Often, they ask in their language, which I don't need to understand to know exactly what they're saying.

I brace myself and shake my head. Gently, slowly, to telegraph regret,

TaRessa Stovall

I add the flicker of a sad smile and gently break the bad news: "No. I'm not." Sometimes I thank them to acknowledge that they have honored me with their hope. And I feel horrible for hours afterward remembering how the spark in their eyes died with my words, the ways that their faces moved from expectation to disappointment, and the sudden chill that replaced the warm rush of expectation. I don't always explain my true background; I've learned the hard way that they don't want to know what I really am. Nothing I say can make up for the letdown I've caused them to feel.

The second beholder is the one who assumes. Like Ms. Gonzales, they classify me according to whatever I most resemble in the database of their life experience. Then they interact with me based on that assumption without ever considering that they could be wrong. It doesn't occur to them to ask.

The assuming beholders arrogantly proclaim, "Oh, you're such-and-such." When I correct them, they argue, as if I can't possibly know more about my own parentage than whatever they're imagining. No matter how clearly I explain my background, the assuming beholders are too hooked on feeling superior to concede to the truth.

Some of these beholders assume I'm White. Obviously, not every person who is racially or ethnically ambiguous-looking physically "qualifies" to be mistaken for White. But for those who do, this adds yet another dimension to navigate in daily life.

While some People of Color have assumed I'm White, that is more the exception than the rule. As for White people, that depends on geography. White people in the Northern, Western, and Midwestern parts of the USA are the most likely to think I'm White. They might ask if I'm Greek, Italian, etc. to quantify my place in the White hierarchy based on immigrant assimilation patterns. When I tell them what I am, their faces scrunch into masks of disbelief, sparking a frenzy of anxious questions to help them relieve the dissonance I am causing them to experience.

White people in the Southern USA are another story. A true Southern White person does not mistake me for White or anything close to it. They have a high level of race-dar encoded in their DNA from plantation days, when a single drop of Black blood had to be visually discernable to identify non-White bodies as property, capital, and collateral. There are zero questions in their brains or eyes, and to them, I'm not even ambiguous-looking. All they see is a light-skinned Black person, case closed.

The third category is the beholders who wonder. Their eyes are full of questions. They appraise every aspect of my appearance: melanin, hair textures, the scope and placement of facial features, body type, body language, etc. They're also scanning hairstyles, clothing, and accessories for clues, while obsessively analyzing my speech patterns and word choices. It's easy to see their minds shorting out, and they desperately strain to fit me into a category to normalize their brain function and quell their anxiety.

For years, I entertained myself by making the wondering beholders guess, since their answers told me more about them than they realized—where they'd grown up, lived and traveled. After I got tired of the game, I told them the truth, amused by the relief on their faces. I recently learned that my brother Greg had done the same thing. We still compare notes about how we're perceived and received in different places and situations.

A few instances of clashes with beholders stand out. The first was in the late 1980s when New York friends took me to visit the famed Sounds of Brazil nightclub, called SOBs. A Latin band was jamming, and we were digging the intricate dance patterns executed on the floor. A brown-skinned man with an Afro extended his hand for me to dance. I followed him onto the dance floor, confident that I could follow him and fake the funk for at least one song. With Ntozake Shange's classic for colored girls… line about how she'd been "twirlin, hippin, givin much quick feet and bein a mute, cute, colored Puerto Rican," on my mind, I looked to my dance partner for cues. He looked back at me for the same thing. Realizing that he probably wasn't Afro-Latino, I stole a glance at the folks dancing next to us so I could copy their steps. Just when I started to pick up the beat, my partner stopped moving, looked me up and down and said, "Wait a minute! You're not even Puerto Rican!" in a voice dripping with disgust. I burst out laughing and said, "Well, neither are you, brothah!" and sashayed back to my seat. While I was amused, I was also frustrated, thinking for the umpteenth time how much simpler life would be if my outsides more accurately reflected my insides.

Incidents with beholders occurred no matter where I lived. In 1991, I was in my late thirties, a newlywed, and hugely pregnant with our son. We'd moved from Atlanta to Washington, D.C., where I'd take a daily walk around the posh Georgetown neighborhood that was our temporary home.

It was February, near the end of the Persian Gulf War, and an interesting time to be in the nation's capital. Before then, I didn't have much experience with being mistaken for Arab. In the first incident, a young White woman cashier handed me an Arabic-language newspaper when I bought a bottle of water from her kiosk. "What's this for?" I asked, confused. "It's free," she smiled encouragingly. "Go ahead, take it." I looked at her strangely and walked away, leaving the newspaper untouched on the counter.

But the assuming beholders can be dangerous, too. A week later, I was crossing a busy Georgetown intersection when a group of young White men shoved my seven-months-pregnant body to the ground. Passersby averted their eyes and rushed past as the group of young men taunted me for being a "fucking Arab terrorist," and spit on the pavement near my face. The light changed, and I struggled to my feet, drivers honking angrily as I stumbled to the curb. That was the first time I felt unsafe and helpless in the face of peoples' assumptions. I spent most of the rest of my pregnancy indoors.

The most consistently unnerving and potentially threatening type of beholder incidents have taken place in airports. Decades before 9/11 led to the formation of the Transportation Security Agency (TSA) and its more stringent security measures, airports were a precarious and unpredictable place for me. On my first visit to Jamaica in the late 1970s, the Customs guys in the airport wouldn't let me into their country until I answered their brusque, "What are you, anyway?" Never mind that they held my U.S. passport in their hands; I knew they weren't asking about my nationality. I gestured to a photo of then-Prime Minister Michael Manley—who was very light-skinned and ambiguous-looking—on the wall behind them and said, "The same as your leader, Prime Minister Manley." Only then did they grant me entry.

In my twenties and thirties, I'd vacationed in various parts of Mexico a few times with no real issues. In the late 1980s, I was re-entering the country through the Dallas, Texas, airport. As I reached the Customs line, a young Mexican woman looked me over for a long, tense minute, then asked me in English, "Where are you from?"

"Se-at-tle," I said, drawing each syllable out in the flattest voice I could manage. I knew she was going to hit the button beneath her counter before she did it. Suddenly I was surrounded by half a dozen huge, intimidating White men. They shouted at me to follow them into a small room. I handed them my passport, which they glanced at and threw aside. They grabbed my suitcase and emptied it to inspect the contents, all the while firing questions at me about where I was born, how many languages I spoke, and where I really lived.

"I'm a Black American," I said as calmly as I could manage, handing them my business card from Spelman College and wondering if I should belt out the Black National Anthem, "Lift Ev'ry Voice and Sing." They continued to interrogate me until I feared that they would take me into some kind of custody. Just when I thought all was lost, a Black man in an airport uniform walked past. In desperation, I waved him over. "Can you please tell these gentlemen that I am Black?" I showed him my Spelman business card. "You know,

African American? Please?"

He looked at my business card, gave me the once-over, and then nodded curtly to the security force. They reluctantly walked away, leaving me to re-pack my suitcase, heart pounding. Once again, I gave thanks that a Black person was willing to stand for my truth when my appearance alone wouldn't suffice.

That 1980s airport experience was just a warm-up for the ongoing delights of TSA since 2001. In the early days after 9/11, I wore my hair to my shoulders. The folks at TSA lit up when they saw me coming (and this was strictly for domestic travel). They took extra special care to pat me down for several minutes at a time, to put that explosive-detecting solution on my hands, to ask detailed questions about my travel plans. They seemed to take great pleasure in digging into my hair to see what I might have hidden there.

Once, when I was traveling with my children, we were waiting to go through an especially long security line. Calvin II asked why so many fellow passengers were staring hard at me as they inched away from us, fear evident on their faces. "Because they think I'm Arab," I said, loudly enough for the staring people to hear.

"No, they don't!" Mariah protested, as several of the people nodded their heads and moved even further away from us. When we got to the security line, the TSA officers grabbed both kids, pulled our bags from the conveyer belt onto the ground and patted us all down for so long that another TSA officer stopped, shook his head, and said, "I've never seen us do that to small children." I've worn my hair very short since then. Needless to say, I've had fewer problems now that I purchased TSA Pre-Check. But that birth certificate is still wedged firmly into my passport cover, and I can never exhale until I'm at my gate.

One of my few regrets as a parent is saddling my son and daughter with being racially ambiguous-looking. Although I can try to help them navigate the dynamics of racial ambiguity, I cannot control how other people will respond and react to them. And I have no way to ease the inconvenience and intrusiveness of it all. It's exhausting and sometimes terrifying to always be on guard, wondering how and when people will project their hopes, assumptions, and questions onto you. It can become an unwelcome distraction to manage when you're just trying to go about your daily business. And it further complicates the already overwhelming dynamics of everyday racism and colorism.

The reality is that ambiguous-looking people are human inkblots.

TaRessa Stovall

Like the Rorschach test where psychologists and therapists show people black ink blots on white paper to analyze their psychological state, the things that people, hope, assume, or wonder reveal less about us, the inkblots, than the people who are looking at us and interacting with what they believe they see.

The biggest downside of racial ambiguity is its unpredictability. It's not as straightforward and easily understood as light-skinned privilege, which manifests in fairly consistent and predictable ways. Ambiguity might help protect me or increase the risk of danger. The toughest part is never knowing. It's hard to assess a threat when I can't tell which direction it's coming from or when it might appear. Any random person could tag me a friend or an enemy. And the truth isn't always an effective means of protection.

I have never wanted to be anything other than what I am. But I have often wished for the simplicity of having people know my heritage, and that of my brother, son and daughter, at first glance. Then they can like us, hate us, embrace us, or reject us based on who we really are, instead of putting us at the mercy of their uncertainty or assumptions.

Chapter 37: What Did You Call Me, Mr. President?

The mid-2000s were defined by unexpected peaks and valleys. Between working at The Montclair Times newspaper, helping Mom navigate her cancer care, and single-parenting two teenagers, I was stretched in several directions. Mom's transition to our boisterous household didn't go as smoothly as either of us had hoped. She was depressed and fearful about her declining health, and I was overwhelmed with guilt and grief, struggling to make things better while both of our hearts were breaking.

She complained that the kids and I "talked too much about race" at the dinner table. I didn't know how to explain the Herculean task of trying to grow healthy, happy, successful Black children in the twenty-first century. I was proud that Calvin II, Mariah, and I were able to openly discuss issues around identity, racism, colorism, and being racially ambiguous-looking. I loved that they were forming their own opinions about themselves and the world around them. While I tried hard to help Mom feel more included in the conversations, I knew they were a world apart from the "people are just people" philosophy she'd shared with Greg and me decades before.

Mom struggled valiantly to beat her cancer, but succumbed to the battle just before Mother's Day 2008. We held two memorial services for Mom—one with close family in Minneapolis, and a larger one in Seattle where Greg, sister Shirley, and our children gathered to scatter her ashes in a river on Mount Rainier. We then celebrated her life with a memorial service and meal with dozens of her friends at an upscale downtown Seattle hotel.

As the keeper of Mom's computer and email, I was able to invite her friends and co-workers, most of whom had never met Greg or me. Though ready to collapse from grief and exhaustion, I managed to speak a few words, which included some Afrocentric blessings. Some of my Black friends, garbed in West African clothing, supported me with "Ashe!" I briefly wondered what the crowd thought of this touch, but was too focused on not collapsing into a puddle of endless tears to give it serious thought.

When Greg stood up to speak after me, he had the good sense to read the room much better than I had. Realizing that many of the guests—especially those who hadn't known that our mother had married a Black man and had Mixed children—might have found the African references strange, he smiled and explained, "I guess I should tell you that TaRessa's always been Black. That's just the way she is."

In that moment, I appreciated my baby brother's insightful diplomacy more than I could say. And I marveled how, even in the saddest time of my entire life, identity always had a way of making itself known.

During Mom's last days, people were gushing over Barack Obama, this "fine, brilliant brother who could be the first Black president." Since I didn't believe such a creature could exist, I looked him up. He checked the predictable boxes for popularity: light-skinned, Ivy League-educated, eloquent in the way that moved Black and White folks alike—but still a political unicorn. I gave him points for being intriguing, but doubted that he had a shot at the White House in 2008.

My heart sank when I found out he was Biracial. The last thing I needed was a reason for people to start publicly dissecting and discussing his heritage and, by extension, mine. I wasn't ready for the demands that would place on my very limited time and energy. This Obama guy's ascent threatened to yank the lid off the long-buried identity battles that I'd tucked away as too complicated and problematic to untangle amid my overwhelming family and work responsibilities. I still proudly claimed all of my heritage, but had become comfortable doing so within the context of Black allegiance and identity. I truly did not need this political upstart threatening my longtime comfort zone, especially as I grieved the loss of my mother.

But this tall, skinny Biracial guy with the big ears and politically incorrect name had a presence that couldn't be denied. While I wasn't as enamored of him as many of the folks—Black and White—around me, I was intrigued. When he beat Hillary Clinton to become the Democratic candidate, I started to take him seriously.

The popular description of Mr. Obama as "the son of a White woman from Kansas and a Black man from Kenya," annoyed the hell out of me, because I felt the sexual fetishizing and "jungle fever" fantasies of that particular kind of interracial mixing behind those words. When he didn't say or do anything that rocked the Mixed-race identity boat, I gradually relaxed my suspicions and became cautiously optimistic about the possibility of him winning the presidency. While I still wished that he wasn't Bi-racial, I noted that, ironically, America probably wasn't ready for any other kind of candidate to run for the title of First Black President.

It was his wife, Michelle, who ultimately won me over. I knew that he couldn't have gotten elected with a wife who was White or a light-skinned woman of any background. His spouse had a style that felt familiar enough to break through most of my reservations. Driven as much by an aversion to the McCain/Palin ticket as the hope that Barack Obama might be good for the country, I did things I'd never done for any candidate: volunteered, displayed yard signs, and donated money at every opportunity. While maintaining a healthy degree of political cynicism, I found his "hope and change" party line a refreshing alternative to the stale status quo.

And I wanted him to win, not so much for me, but for Calvin II and Mariah and all young People of Color. I loved the idea that they could see themselves reflected in the leader of the free world. On voting day, I continued the family tradition of taking the kids to the polls, emphasizing the historical importance of casting a ballot. Even as I hoped he'd win, I had zero faith that the USA would make him their choice.

I was pleasantly shocked at his victory—running into the streets to dance and shout with joy, yet still incredulous. I had never for a single moment believed that the United States would elect this man to run the country. I knew his presidency wouldn't end racism, but it felt strangely wonderful to allow myself to believe that the election of President Barack Hussein Obama signaled the possibility of progress. Thoughts of what this might mean to generations of ancestors and the problematic racial history of our nation made me tear up with emotion.

My euphoria didn't last long.

Days after the election, I eagerly tuned into the nightly network news for the new President-elect's very first news conference. The eyes and ears of the world were upon him, as he described promising his daughters Sasha and Malia that they could get a dog if they won the White House.

The new President-elect, relaxed and smiling, shared that Malia's allergies would impact their choice of a pet. "There are a number of breeds that are hypoallergenic, but on the other hand, our preference is to get a shelter dog, but obviously, a lot of the shelter dogs are mutts like me."

I'd been sweeping the kitchen floor. At the words "mutts like me," I dropped the broom, scattering the dirt I'd just swept up. "I can't believe it," I shouted. "He just called himself a mutt. A dog. This is a whole different level of wrong. The first Mixed-Black President-elect of the United States of America's very first words to the world are to insult himself and all Mixed people."

At that moment, I recognized that all of my apprehension about this Mixed-race man had been justified. While others might have processed him calling himself a "mutt" as a cute, self-deprecating quip to reassure everyone that he prioritized his American identity, that term perpetuated and justified the practice of dehumanizing People of Color by labeling us as animals. One of the main problems with the term Mulatto is that it was created to represent the "unnatural" mating of a horse and a donkey. I cringed on behalf of all the young Mixed-race people seeing and hearing the most famous, powerful Biracial person in United States history give the world permission to refer to us as animals. I pictured Mixed kids being called "mutt" by others, and when they protested, their tormentors justifying the insult with "President Obama said it, so I can too."

I didn't sleep that night, my mind racing. Because beyond my anger at the new President-elect, my inner voice suggested that maybe the despicable phrase, "a mutt like me" was a gift, a catalyst, a sign for me to pay attention to advocating for a healthy Mixed-race identity again. I can't, I argued. I was several months and many dollars into a promising media venture with a group of friends. I wasn't going to forsake that to chase some dream from my youth, especially one that nobody else seemed to care about.

I teetered between balancing my disappointment at the First Black President's "mutt" moment and enthusiastically celebrating his political victory. The rational part of my mind recognized that he was being calling himself a "mutt" to help make America more comfortable with his background. Maybe he was alluding to the popular notion that most Americans are racial or ethnic "mutts"—a swipe at the fantasy of racial purity. But the part of me that had spent my whole life starving for even a single representation that felt honest and strong and proud and true felt betrayed. The part of me that worried from the first moment I'd learned he was Mixed knew he wouldn't fulfill those needs of mine. I'd just been blindsided by him deliberately slurring his background—and by extension, the backgrounds of myself and so many others—in the public arena. We're often encouraged or required to put sacrifice our self-respect by putting ourselves down to make others comfortable, downplaying the possibility of liking ourselves because that is too much for America to digest. His "mutt" comment devastated me not because I was unable to see the nuances in the messaging. It devastated me because I could.

I prayed that the new president-elect would never utter another public word about his identity. I didn't have the bandwidth to entertain the Militant Mixedness of my youth, which threatened to bust out of the corner I'd boxed it into if he continued to denigrate himself—and us—from his platform of commander in chief.

The kids and I traveled to Washington, D.C., to experience his historic inauguration on a freezing January day. Every time I saw him on television, it felt like a dream, too good to be true. I was cool with him as long as he never again referenced his identity.

At this time, people my age were starting to get on Facebook. I reluctantly joined, knowing I needed to learn about this strange new thing called social media. At first, it was a chore, and I couldn't see what all the hype was about. After a while, I noticed some Mixed-race groups. Curious, I joined to see what they were talking about. I fell into a whole new world of younger Mixed people throwing around terms like "admixture," "hypodescent," and "phenotype," while some of them challenged the long-held notion of the One-Drop Rule that designated anyone with known or discernable Black ancestry as Black. I read, questioned, and debated in these groups, fascinated by these fresh views and perspectives. I was intrigued by the hint of a place—even if it was strictly digital—where Mixed identity could be explored and explained by us, for us, uninterrupted by the voices of others.

My planned business venture with friends fell through—our capabilities weren't in line with either our ambitions or the time it would take to bring them to fruition. Though I wasn't ready to jump on a Mixed-pride bandwagon, conversations inside and outside of the Mixed groups on Facebook caused me to reconsider the dynamics of racial identity in these intriguing new spaces.

Then came the 2010 Census, with lots of publicity about its groundbreaking option for Mixed people. But when I saw the form, it was the same misguided, dismissive "Some Other Race" terminology as back in 2000. Perhaps if the language had been more respectful and specific, I'd have considered the existence of that box a sign of some progress. But that, plus awareness of how the resulting data would be used, made checking the "Black" box a no-brainer.

President Obama's decision to check the "Black" box received a fair amount of media coverage and fueled long exchanges on social media. Some Mixed-race people were disappointed, viewing it as a sign that he'd chosen his Blackness over his Mixedness. Many Black people shared the longtime attitude that anyone with Black blood was Black, period, point blank. That moment, coupled with my now-enthusiastic use of social media to process these dynamics, had me thinking more deeply about the ways in which Black and Mixed-race identities are often set up to conflict with each other. When popular celebrities like Halle Berry said publicly that they considered themselves Black, the conversations reignited. No matter how passionately people presented their opinions on the topic, it was clear that these exchanges were stuck in endless loops of sparring with no effort to move beyond this deadlocked dialogue to a more inclusive acceptance of Mixed identity in its many variations.

Meanwhile, Calvin II and Mariah challenged my identity with ideas about their own. I'd reared them to know that they were Black with a Mixed mother and a Jewish Baubie. Three of their four grandparents were Black. Yes, they were light-skinned, with all the attendant privilege that entails the dynamics of which I'd tried to prepare them to process and navigate as they matured.

We talked openly about identity. When we saw Biracial celebrities having children, we discussed whether they were "Halle Berry" babies—three-quarters White, or "Malia and Sasha Obama" types—who were three-quarters Black.

Somewhere in these conversations, my children talked about visiting various after-school clubs in their diverse high school: the Jewish club, the Mixed-race club, etc. "That's cool," I smiled. "But you're not Mixed."

They said I was wrong, sparking months of heated debates. "Mixed means that you have parents of two different races," I insisted. "Like me."

"That's not all it is," they countered. "You don't get it!"

We went in circles with this conversation until I saw people in some of my Mixed-race Facebook groups throwing around a new term: MGM, which meant Multi-generational Mixed, for people who had one or more Mixed parents.

While it challenged what I believed and the way I moved through the world, I felt the ding of truth in this category. Mixed folks had been around for centuries. Why wouldn't there be a way to describe our children?

With a shock, I realized I'd been identity policing my own son and daughter, just as the world had so often done to me and to them. While I'd insisted that "the first step to empower yourself is to define yourself," I'd disputed their right to define themselves. I wasn't supporting my own in taking that very step. I realized I'd been the worst kind of hypocrite.

I was flooded with deep shame that I'd resisted my own children's attempts to do the very thing I'd always fought for. I'd been so smug in my certainty that I could help them navigate the treacherous waters of racism, colorism, ambiguous appearances, and identity that I'd dismissed their efforts to define themselves. I'd become what I'd hated for so long: someone who policed other people's identities. And I'd wielded the same weapons against my own children that had been used to keep me in my place.

"I am so sorry," I said to them, once my head cleared. "You're right, and I'm wrong. You have the right to determine your own identity. I hope you can forgive me one day."

It was then that I revisited the Militant Mixed self I'd set aside years before. I heeded the whispers that President Obama's problematic "mutt like me" phrase was a signal to dust off my youthful dream to do something that might help the world to move beyond the "danger of the single story" that Nigerian novelist Chimamanda Ngozi Adichie had made famous in her TEDx Talk.

That "single story" of being Mixed-race has been that of the Tragic Mulatto. This has been the only public representation and defining narrative of anyone who was an obvious mix of Black and anything else, particularly White, in the United States. That stereotype persists, even in contemporary times, despite the fact that most Black-White Mixed people are now created through consensual unions rather than from the rapes of enslavement. It isn't hard to see that "tragic" refers to the idea of being so close to, yet so far away from, Whiteness with all of its power and advantage. Of course, it assumes White superiority and Black inferiority. And it negates the idea of a Mixed-with-Black person having any agency over his or her identity or place in the world, or any options beyond the rigid Black-White binary.

The truth is, the singular "tragedy" of being Mixed-race is racism--the source of pain and suffering for anyone who isn't deemed White by birth or assimilation. Racism is genuinely tragic for everyone on the receiving end of its non stop oppression, injustice, and inequality. While the specifics of the impact can vary based on bloodlines, appearance, geography, and other details, the overall dynamic remains the same. As long as this "tragedy" is focused on Mixed people rather than all People of Color impacted by racism, it's dangerously easy to be distracted from the true nature of this beast and the insidious ways in which it impacts us all.

My identity journey has shown me that there are several factors involved in how Mixed people's identities evolve and are viewed by ourselves and by others. They are: ancestry, atmosphere (the environment in which one's identity is formed), appearance, affinity for one or more cultures, affiliation with one or more groups and cultures, and allegiance to one or more groups or cultures. Groups and cultures include race, ethnicity, nationality, religion, tribe, and other identity markers.

The pressure that many folks who aren't Mixed feel to neatly categorize our messy identities sometimes leads to the misconception that we're "confused." The truth is that more people are confused about us than we are about ourselves. They project their confusion onto us, and it becomes part of the brand, the stereotype that we are clueless and must be schooled about our lives, often by people who have no idea what we think, feel, or experience. This urge for easy categorization can cause conflicts between people wanting to label us, and we the Mixed people whose realities are often more nuanced and complex than the standard construct of "either-or" acknowledges.

Make no mistake: racial identity in the USA is always contentious and fraught with tensions. Especially when Blackness is part of the mix. None of these things can be understood or processed outside of the context of systemic racism. Sometimes we Mixed folks naturally internalize these tensions around identity. These tensions can also show up in family dynamics and in the ways that we are received, perceived, and considered in the larger society.

All of this contributes to what I call "Identity Policing," which happens when someone from one group tells someone from another group what they are or aren't, and how their identity works or should work. Identity Policing is based on the premise that someone who is not you is somehow qualified to judge or determine your identity for their own purposes. People of all races do it to those they deem "other." Mixed people are by no means the only targets of Identity Policing but, depending on how our specific mix relates to the demographics of the environment we're in, many people feel entitled to question our identities, challenge them, and sometimes try to override our truths with their assumptions and biases. I've even seen Mixed people Identity Policing each other. These are unfortunate but natural outcomes in a society built, based, and run on racist determinants and categories designed to foster inequality, exclusion, and conflict.

As is the case with many Mixed people, my existence and my appearance still inspire strong--sometimes extreme--responses, along with endless questions and challenges. These things have shaped so much of my life—too much of it, really. I've spent decades wrestling with the best way to define myself on my own terms. None of this is easy or comfortable.

Throughout my life, people have asked why I have such a strong sense of my racial identity. When I was young, I thought that was the case for all Mixed people, especially since it seemed to be among most of those in my community. But people of different races repeatedly said that my identity dynamics stood out to them. I didn't know how to answer or respond to them.

I believe the Jazz Baby community that my mother and the other interracially-married women worked to create made a difference because growing up in that context enabled us to understand our backgrounds as normal. I think that vaccinated us with levels of confidence to help us to navigate the questions and challenges to our identities in the larger world. I know it did for me.

More than anything, I have to credit my mother, Rosalyn Weisberg Stone. By standing proud and strong in her truth, and living with uncompromising integrity, she inspired Greg and I to determine our own truths, and stand in them, even when those truths weren't popular or politically expedient. By teaching us that we had to face ourselves honestly in the mirror, Mom prepared us for the realities of a world that wasn't always ready or welcoming. Mom didn't only speak Yiddish and Jazz, she lived the synthesis. By embodying the "and," she enabled Greg and I to do the same. She moved through the world in a way that armored us against the many forms of confusion we would encounter, and protected us from internalizing it or taking it personally.

Mixed-race people in the United States are born into a maze of structural -isms and pressured to form a sense of self between the rock of systemic racism and the hard place of ever-shifting rules and identifiers. We're often pushed to "choose" between the groups we're born into to ease the discomfort that some people feel because we exist. We're visible reminders of boundaries crossed and rules broken. Some see us as a threat to their purity, others as a form of genocide, an erasure of their future existence.

I came of age as the nation grappled with its bloody history and the ubiquitous brutality of "race relations." I came of race during a bold chapter in the struggle for human rights. As language shifted and terminology evolved, I struggled to be recognized in my entirety and accepted for my truth. I have never been confused about my identity. Unlike many Mixed people, my sense of self has not been shaped by feeling rejected by the groups represented in my ancestry. Despite some people's view that I could or should exploit my ambiguous appearance "to be anything I want," I have never wanted to be anything but what I am.

For the first time in my life and perhaps in this country's history, there are ongoing public conversations about racial identity in general and about Mixed identity in particular. Because racism causes endless wounds, trauma, conflicts, and divisions, many discussions around these issues are contentious. Compounding the problem is the fact that there is no agreement about the terminology to be used in having these exchanges, because every single term is deemed problematic by some people, and all of the terms are locked and loaded in some way. Sometimes we can't fully engage in real conversations because we're so busy disagreeing about our preferred terms and how we define and apply them. But maybe it doesn't make sense to expect or strive for consensus. Nothing about identity leads to the comfort of tidy conclusions.

I don't know the answers, but this Mixed life has taught me the value of exploring the questions in all of their painful, difficult complexity. Not everyone wants to have these conversations since they can be triggering, frustrating, and exhausting. This is understandable, as so many people with Black ancestry live with profound, usually multi-generational, trauma around our backgrounds, histories, and identities. Still, my experiences keep me committed to posing the questions and prompting these conversations because, as James Baldwin taught us, "Not everything we face can be changed. But nothing can be changed until it is faced."

Obviously, I don't have the solutions to systemic racism and its side effects. But my Ancestors trust and compel me to do my part to challenge those evils. I believe that we can best fight in a collective way, with the unity and solidarity that prioritize our common goals. I also know that there is power in the specificity that each of us brings to the collective, so that we continue to enrich each other.

Mixed-race identity--especially when it includes Black--is inherently controversial in a society that manipulates race in service to power and domination. While more Mixed-race children than ever before are being born, the questions around our conception and existence persist. Not everyone wants to acknowledge the multi-faceted diversity inherent in our presence. We are not a monolith, and even the ever-changing ways that the U.S. government strives to label, contain, and predict our presence cannot force us into a single story.

Some Mixed people fit neatly into the designations to which we are assigned. Others don't naturally conform, but will contort, maim, or even amputate parts of themselves to fit in. And some have the audacity to try to live tabout who we are and where we find our sense of self, purpose, and community along the way.

In the process, we learn how to resist those things that threaten our humanity and our right to thrive. In honor of our Ancestors and for the love of our Descendants, the battle cry continues: A luta continua! As long as racism plagues our country, the struggle shall endure.

The 2010 Census

Current census questionnaires used a two-question format to ask U.S. residents about their race and Hispanic ethnicity. First, they were asked whether they are of Hispanic, Latino, or Spanish origin and, if so, whether it is Mexican, Puerto Rican, Cuban, or another Hispanic origin.

The next question asked about race. The 2010 options were:

White; Black, African American or Negro; American Indian or Alaska Native; and several Asian options including Indian, Chinese, Filipino, Japanese, Korean, Vietnamese, Native Hawaiian, Samoan, or Other Pacific Islander.

Again, as in 2000, is the option "Some Other Race" at the bottom like an afterthought, with instructions to "print race" in the boxes below.

A look at how the U.S. government keeps shifting, adapting, and sometimes redefining identity categories over the decades reveals this nation's continual quest to group people for the benefit of those in power. Census options increasingly reflect some groups pushing to be categorized and counted differently.

The 2020 Census

The 2020 Census will offer people the option to choose from among 15 racial categories. For the first time, individuals will also be able to identify their ethnic or national origin as part of the race question. The main racial categories are White; Black or African Am.; American Indian or Alaska Native; Chinese; Filipino; Asian Indian; Vietnamese; Korean; Japanese; Native Hawaiian; Samoan; Chamorro; Other Asian; and Other Pacific Islander. There is also the option to write in races not included on the form.

As for the "Some Other Race" category in the 2000 Census-- the first time it was offered--about 2 percent of Americans chose more than one race. In the 2010 Census, about 3 percent selected that option.

On one hand, humans are, as my mother stubbornly insisted, "just people." On the other hand, a look at the U.S. census across the decades reveals the government's continual quest to label folks in a way that can shape our sense of self while controlling the flow of resources that impact our options, opportunities, and quality of life.

Public conversations about racial identity are taking place as never before. With the browning of the USA and the predicted growth of the Mixed-race population, they are likely to continue challenging all of us to define who we are in relation to our Ancestors, ourselves, and each other.

In this process, each of us has our own roads to travel, our own challenges to wrestle, and our own truths to tell.

Thank you for taking the time to consider mine.

Credits and Permissions:

Census information from "Racial Categories Used in the Decennial Census, 1970 to the Present" by Claudette E. Bennnett, Branch Chief, Racial Statistics Branch, Population Division, U.S. Bureau of the Census.

Excerpt from The Autobiography of Malcolm X as Told to Alex Haley, Ballantine Books, 1964

Excerpt from Soledad Brother: The Prison Letters of George Jackson, by George L. Jackson, Bantam Books, Inc., 1972

Context:

To help put my identity journey into a broader context, I am sharing relevant findings from the Pew Research Center on Multiracial people in the USA. In 2015, the Pew Research Center conducted the first major survey of Multiracial people in the USA from a nationally representative sample of 1,555 Multiracial Americans ages 18 and older.

First, the big picture. Based on census data, the Pew Research Center states in "Race and Multiracial Americans in the U.S. Census," that:

- The U.S. population of two-race ancestry has more than doubled in size, from about 5.1 million in 1980 to 13.5 million in 2012.

- According to the U.S. Census Bureau, about nine million Americans—or 6.9 percent of the population—chose two or more racial categories when asked about their race in 2013. Of that 6.9 percent, 2.6 percent described their Multiracial background based on their grandparents; 2.9 percent based on their parents; and 1.4 percent chose "two or more races" based on themselves.

- Between 2000 and 2010, when the census included the "Some Other Race" option, the number of Black–White Biracial Americans more than doubled, while Asian–White Biracial Americans increased by 87 percent.

- The share of Multiracial babies has grown from 1 percent in 1970 to 10 percent in 2013.

The mixes themselves are shifting. Nearly seven percent of U.S. adults have at least two races in their background based on races of self, parents, or grandparents:

- 50 percent are American Indian–White
- 12 percent are American Indian-Black
- 11 percent are Black-White
- 11 percent are Multiracial Hispanic
- 6 percent are White-Black-American Indian
- 5 percent are some other combination

While Multiracial adults share some things in common, they cannot be easily categorized. Their experiences and attitudes differ significantly depending on the races that make up their background and how the world sees them. The Pew Research Center survey found that:

- About 60 percent of respondents say they felt proud to be Multiracial, and 59 percent feel more open to other cultures.
- About 30 percent say they have changed the way they describe their race over the years, with some saying they once thought of themselves as only one race and now think of themselves as more than one race, and others saying the opposite.
- A majority—55 percent—say they have been subjected to racial slurs or jokes.
- Multiracial adults with a Black background report experiences with discrimination that closely mirror those of single-race Blacks.
- A quarter—25 percent—say people are "often or sometimes confused by their racial background."
- About 24 percent have felt annoyed because people have made assumptions about their racial background.

Is being Multiracial an advantage or a disadvantage? While 19% of all Multiracial adults say it has been an advantage, 76% say it has not made a difference. Of those who say that it is an advantage:

- 58 percent are Asian–White
- 25 percent are Black–White
- 22 percent are Black–American Indian–White
- 14 percent are American Indian–White
- 10 percent are Black–American Indian

Multiracial identity is complicated:

- Only 39 percent of Multiracial adults say they consider themselves to be Mixed-race or Multiracial.
- 61 percent say they don't consider themselves to be Multiracial.
- 70 percent who are White and Asian say they identify as Multiracial
- 61 percent who are Black and White say they identify as Multiracial
- 25 percent of those who are American Indian and White say they identify as Multiracial
- About 21 percent of all the Multiracial adults surveyed say they have felt pressured from friends, family, or "society in general" to identify as a single race.

Those who are Black–White:

"It's not so much the experience of what you've been through, but it's the way you weave your memory."

Romare Bearden, African American artist, writer 1911 - 1988

Gratitudes

It takes a village to raise a book. All of my deepest gratitude, appreciation, and thanks go to everyone who lifted me up and held me down and made this insanely challenging five-year journey possible:

First and foremost, my parents, Rosalyn Weisberg Stone and George Kelly Stone, and all of the Ancestors whose lives made mine a reality and whose journeys informed and inspired my own.

My Baby Bro, Gregory Stone, and my Big Sis, Shirley Aaron, for being my anchors, my oars, and my lighthouses on the seas of this life.

My son, Calvin, and my daughter, Mariah, first, for making me a mother. And second, for early reads and fundraising assistance—I truly could not have done this without your wisdom, talent, support, and inspiration.

My lifelong friends who are with me to this day, and whose presence has been pivotal in my evolution: Celia King, Linda (Steinmann) Eschels, Karen Davis, and Michelle Fields, and John Vallot.

The childhood friends who have made their transitions. I eagerly await our reunions on the other side: Carolyn Wells, Sheryl Paul Colvin, and Yolaine Vallot.

The men who saw a spark and invested in me throughout my youth: Ed Samuelsson, Larry Gossett, and Elmer Dixon, Aaron Dixon, and the Seattle Chapter of the Black Panther Party for Self-Defense. Your examples of living activism, caring, and concern set the template for what I knew was possible in life.

My dear friend, mentor and former professor, Dr. Joye Hardiman, who planted the seed for this book decades ago when she said that I had to write "the story of how a colored girl became a Black woman who always honored her Jewish mother." And Dr. Maxine Mimms for demonstrating the power of community and pushing me to find my voice.

Sherry Bennett, for awesome decades of friendship, and for the beauty and power of moving through the world in your truth.

Janell Walden Agyeman, who worked so diligently to help pull this book together.

My fabulous editor and publishing partner, Donald Brooks Jones and his team at Alchemy Media Publishing. Y'all rock!

Dr. Stacey Patton, for endless inspiration and fearless fire.

Iya Jo Anna Hunter, for spiritual guidance, wisdom, and sistergirl-friend riches.

Andrea Ivory for support in endless forms.

President Barack H. Obama for getting on my nerves in a way that forced me to write this down and get it out into the world.

The late, great literary queen Gwendolyn Brooks, who read my youthful poems and responded with genuine encouragement to make me believe I could really be a writer.

My awesome beta readers, whose constructive criticism, insights, and candid feedback drove several revisions: Joye Mercer Barksdale, Lisa Williamson Rosenberg, Ayanna Bennett Meyers, and Michelle Collison.

Extra kudos to Ayanna for awesome proofreading.

The folks in my many Mixed-race and Jews of Color Facebook groups for keeping me thinking, questioning, and growing.

The staff of Seattle Public Schools and the U.S. Census Bureau who so patiently answered my endless queries.

The very talented Brittni Perkins for my glorious cover art.

The amazing Curtis Bunn and the National Book Club Conference.

The gifted Ella B. Curry and LaShaunda Hoffman for adding your promotional expertise to the mix.

Shirley Mitchell and The Inquirers Club book club of Atlanta, whose loving patience got me through a tough stretch or two—I look forward to our date!

My Muse, who puts me through the paces and always delivers in the clutch.
The Orishas, whose beautiful wisdom, guidance, and power sweeten and strengthen this incarnation as they have in the past. Maferefun!
Everyone who has ever asked me any variation of "What are you?" especially if you challenged my response, attempted to override my truth, or tried to police my identity in any way.

TaRessa Stovall

The amazing contributors to my early crowdfunding campaign - your generosity made this possible:

Sil Lai Abrams, Adam Anik & Donna Indahl, William Anthony, Andrea Ashmore, Maxine Baker, Lary Barilleau, Kathryn Bowser, Cameron Boyle, Monique Brizz-Walker, Patricia Bzdil Paul, Paula Caffey Colony, Kathryn Eddy, Linda Eschels, Dawn Florence, Brunetta Garrard, Emmett Glover, Harvey Greenberg, Jerry Hunnicutt, Kathleen Hunter, Niki Hunter Janay, Rosalind Johnson, ELoiza Jorge, Katherine Joyce, Ama Karikari-Yawson, Abe Kasbo, Angela Lockhart Aronoff, Yvonne Majette, Melanese Marr-Thomas, Susan Newman Moore, Tawnya Pettiford-Wates, Kirsten Ray, Zjien Relician, RLB Roberts, Susan Ross, Chandra Russell, Sarah, Harriet Sanford, Daryl Michael Scott, Tara Spicer, Angela Tompkins, Lisa VPS, Carolyn Wells, Anthony Williams, Lisa Williamson-Rosenberg, Jacques Yerby.

And to my readers: THANK YOU for entrusting me with your valuable time, attention, and energy. This is all for you!

TaRessa Stovall